SURPASS EVERY EXPECTATION

SURPASS EVERY EXPECTATION

A PROVEN SYSTEM FOR HELPING PARENTS
RAISE HIGH ACHIEVING CHILDREN

PAULINE PANI LIMEN

CHALFANT ECKERT

PUBLISHING

1028 S Bishop Avenue, Dept. 178
Rolla, MO 65401

Printed in the United States of America

This book is dedicated to my loving and caring husband William for encouraging and supporting me as I wrote this book and passionately believing in my vision. To my lovely daughters Jemima, Joella and Jessica for their love and encouragement. To my Creator to whom I owe all that I am and all that I have.

TABLE OF CONTENTS

REVIEWS

For a loving parent, the years of a child from birth to maturity are delightful. However, the heavy demands of caring for a child in every facet of their life could be quite challenging but rewarding, more so when the outcomes are positive. Learning the truth about the way in which children learn and achieve requires immense efforts and the ability to set objectives. Parental involvement has become an ever increasing factor to helping a child achieve optimally. This book provides a robust system that will help parents unlock their children's potentials. This book covers concepts that every parent should know in order to improve their child's achievement. Parents must understand the factors that influence pupil achievement. Pauline highlights reasons why students fail to achieve their full potential and offers very practical strategies to help parents support their children's studies.

This book is very informative and every parent and educator should read it. It provides parents and guardians with the tools needed to guide their children and instil habits that will help them achieve every goal or objective they set themselves as the go through life. As a mother of four children, I now have clear methods I can use to engage my children and motivate them to excel and become well rounded individuals. This book is a good read and I recommend it to parents, guardians, children's workers and leaders who make key decisions that influence changes in education, families and society.

Irene Tabeth
Head Teacher SOL Academy

Surpass every expectation will encourage you and provoke you to be determined to work with your children to attain the highest that God has purposed for them. The principles are clearly presented, relevant for today and the future and will stir you to action. The strategies can be applied to all areas of life. 'Without a vision my people perish'. The book is practical and enjoyable to read and will bring a change that will spur your children to outstanding heights. I am delighted to recommend this as a 'must read' for every parent that is not satisfied with the minimum but desire the 'very best' for their children.

Dr. Lola Ayoola,
Consultant Paediatrician and Diabetes Lead
Honorary Senior Lecturer
Faculty of Medical and Human Sciences
University of Manchester

. . . .

Surpass every expectation is THE book for parents who are serious about providing their children with the right foundation to maximise their educational capacity. Drawing on relevant scripture, her extensive knowledge of being a teacher and a parent, Pauline Limen offers great context regarding the significance of formal education as a component of the parenting role - challenging the notion that education is the responsibility of the 'system'. The reader is encouraged to align the vision and expectation for their child beyond arbitrary targets set by school. Pauline offers insight into the educational structure and its role as well as the role of parents in developing innate skills, talents and children's interest, leading to an increase in self-esteem and confidence. The book provides very good, easy to follow approaches (such as understanding the learning style of the child, the role of stability, peace and structure in the home and of educating the child on education and developing an entrepreneurial mind set) any parent or guardian can follow. Forming a useful textbook, each chapter is concluded with key questions to encourage reflection and as a call to action, ensuring that parents step fully into their role as collaborators and leaders for their child's educational journey.

Joanna Oliver
CEO ConsultAChameleon

· ·

This book is an amazing, inspiring and well-written book that will empower parents to raise successful offspring. In this day and age when technology has stolen the time parents used to spend with children, this book will revolutionize the way parents think and will help students reach their full potential. I love that the book provides step-by-step instruction on how to help your child succeed. It is a must read for every parent.

Dr Lydie Ndansi
Consultant Endocrinologist
Assistant Professor of Medicine
Associate Program Director of Internal Residency
NSMC, MA

· ·

The book is a must read for parents or future parents providing a vivid, clever, heartfelt, personal, graphic and inspiring description. It prescribes and provides guidelines to parenting, highlighting the disadvantages of bringing up children without taking an active interest in their academic, social and personal growth or paying attention to the company they keep, their lack of discipline and/or motivation. The book talks in-depth about methods that can be used by parents to encourage and motivate children in achieving their potential and excelling in both their academic and social objectives.

The book takes into account reasons such as location, choice of school, home environment, busy professional life, that can play a part in how children turn out. Hence the need to pay attention to the circumstances that might hinder your children. The sentiments echoed as I read encourages parents to share their values of hard work, managing adversity, perseverance, sacrifice, achievement and leadership.

Julian Ebai
Managing Director and Consultant
Jetplay Consulting Ltd

I love this book – *Surpass Every Expectation*. It is simple, straight to the point and exactly what parents need to read, know and implement. Right from the introduction, there is much amazing information. The 3-fold role of a parent: as a Role Model, Teacher and Mentor cannot be under-estimated nor 'un-lived' by parents. Education whether it be that of running one's business or that of formal education cannot be under-stated nor should it be ignored. In fact, if we ignore it, education does not cease, our children are still being educated whether we do so intentionally or not. I am really excited about Surpass Every Expectation because it gives not just the parent direction but the child hope. This book is a MUST read and the nuggets implemented - immediately. I will advise starting from where you are. It might take time but it will pay off. Our children will remember that we were there for them. They will also remember when we were not there for them. You choose.

Kemi Oyesola (Coach Kemi)
Founder of How2Think

FOREWORD

Every parent wants the best for their child – they want to encourage them to succeed and meet their full potential, but not at the detriment of their emotional well-being. In our busy modern lives, we are bombarded by information about raising children, much of it conflicting, and oftentimes it seems that "encouragement" when we are busy - and anxious about which information to trust - can easily slip into frustrated bargaining and ordering; Pauline Limen offers a different way.

This accessible, clear and practical guide is essential reading for the parent that values the positive impact that education and learning, in its widest sense, can have on their child's future success and happiness: the impact that ensures children can meet their potential – not only educationally but also outside the classroom. Both eminently readable but also rigorously researched, Limen's approach is founded on her years of experience as a practitioner and founder of *Star Reachers* – an organization that aims to empower and challenge parents to help their children aspire for academic excellence via practical educational seminars, empowerment seminars and mentoring programmes. This book should be read by parents and teachers alike: working on the basis that a love of learning and the ability to succeed in the modern world is a fascinating matrix of environment, values, context and coaching - the stages of Limen's programme expertly guide parents and educators through these areas of development with warmth, understanding and inspiring pragmatism.

A staunch advocate of drawing on all aspects of a child's environment and daily experiences to help them develop positive skills for learning and life, Limen offers crystal clear actions and questions to help parents reflect on and become actively involved in their child's education. It is a book about developing engaged learners, and creating engaging learning environments for a child, in whatever context they might find themselves. Packed with hints, advice and practical suggestions about learning, relationships and encouragement, this guide book provides an authoritative account of the methods parents can employ to ensure their children flourish as they grow, shoring up both their future success and their future happiness. An inspiring and highly informative must-read for all parents and practitioners caring for children today.

E C Nash MA BEd (hons)
Cantab Head Teacher
Preparatory Department Manchester High School for Girls

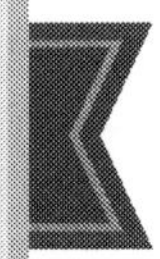

ADDITIONAL FOREWORD

Surpass Every Expectation is a unique resource that addresses a core elements of positive parenting most people do not talk about - the important role of parents in nurturing success in their children and helping to unleash their hidden potentials. In particular, the book's "tri-dimensional" model of parenting for success - the "teacher-model-mentor" approach is a helpful guide for parents to better understand how they could be core drivers of their child's educational attainment. Parents reading this book will gain a rich insight into how to improve their skills to be able to utilise the tri-dimensional model to support their children. The core message I get from reading this book is the role of supportive love in nurturing success in children. This book is not about burdensome or harsh parenting. Many parents would therefore enjoy reading the book and would learn from it.

Debbie Ariyo OBE
Founder and Chief Executive of AFRUCA

PREFACE

The purpose of this book is to equip parents with a range of tools needed to help their children achieve full potential, academic excellence and overall success in life. In my 13 years of Secondary Science teaching experience, I have encountered a wide range of students from varying ethnic backgrounds who were not achieving their full potential. I earnestly knew deep within me that with the right mind set and strategic parental support, these students could achieve a lot more. Student underachievement is an epidemic that has been a major concern within the state school system for decades – I term this phenomenon 'a waste of potential'. The lack of parental involvement or inappropriate parental involvement in their children's education in combination with other factors is a significant contributory factor to pupil underachievement. Interacting with parents as an educator has revealed some interesting findings about the awareness of the need, nature and extent of their involvement in their children's education. Some parents do not see the need to be involved in their children's education; some parents do not know how to help their children do better in school; others have a little understanding of how to support their children's studies and others know how to help children achieve their full potential. Regrettably, a lot of young people's futures are jeopardised by completing school without achieving the required grades needed to access their dream courses in universities of their choice. Parents need HELP with supporting their children's education to break the cycle of underachievement. My greatest motivation for writing this book is my desire for every child regardless of intelligence, ability, ethnic background or social class to achieve their full potential, excel in their studies and succeed in life.

Why the title *Surpass every expectation?* I was inspired to come up with this title because within the educational system, students are set targets or expectations. Parents, children and even educators who lack an understanding of the growth mind-set in learning believe that intelligence and ability are fixed and can't be improved or developed. Active and strategic parental involvement in children's studies will help them surpass every expectation set by the school.

What's the purpose of this book? The topic of parenting is a mine field and parents need as much help as possible to navigate through different aspects of their parenting journey. *Surpass every expectation* is for EVERY parent who wants to raise high achieving children – a topic that for a long time has been very close to my heart. This book is a manual loaded with easy to implement strategies to help parents support children's studies effectively. Extensive research on the impact of parental involvement on pupil achievement reveals that children are best placed to succeed in school when parents are ACTIVELY involved in their studies. The book is full of proven strategies that contribute positively towards my children's future, as well as those of thousands of parents who have listened to me teach them and have sent testimonials across to acknowledge the impact of my work in various aspects of their parenting.

My intention as you read this book is that you will experience a mind-shift and attitude change regarding the issues that can contribute to your child's future success, specifically their education, the development of their gifts, talents, skills, and values as well as the principles of success that will help them develop into happy, fulfilled, confident and well-adjusted adults. I am hoping that you will rise up to the task to get involved in your child's education and see them surpass every expectation, regardless of the labels that may have been placed on them. You have the choice to let life happen to your child or to take charge and impact your child's future positively and help them become the person God had destined them to be.

Each chapter in this book deals with a specific topic followed by a workbook section. Thinking through the questions and writing down the answers will help you to better engage with the content. For optimum benefit, I recommend that you read the book all the way through. Alternatively, you can skip to the particular chapter that you feel is of the most relevance. My most valuable recommendation is to try out the strategies and be consistent with them. Developing new habits has never been a straightforward thing to do, however with persistence, consistency, determination and prayers, you will get your child where you want them to be.

Enjoy the ride as you take on the challenge to help your child surpass every expectation and reach for the stars. There is greatness in your child.

Pauline Pani Limen

ACKNOWLEDGEMENTS

I extend appreciation and thanks to my friends and family for supporting, encouraging and believing in my work and the possibilities that lie ahead and praying for me. Special thanks to my parents Mr and Mrs Pani - especially my father for encouraging me, continually enquiring about the progress of the book and believing in my work. To my wonderful cousin Zac Mbanya for always being available and willing to do the initial editing of the book. To my special friend and accountability partner Jennifer Ndi Nzenyuy whose motivation, encouragement and belief have been of great support during this journey.

INTRODUCTION

Have you ever wondered why your child, who seems so incredibly bright, consistently accomplishes less than you expect? You're not alone! Many parents feel frustrated knowing that their children hold such amazing reserves of untapped potential, and they desperately want to know how to unlock it. They're around their children enough to know that these kids are bright, but may suspect they are underperforming in school simply because they are unchallenged. Who is to blame? Like many parents, you may be putting the responsibility solely on the teacher.

In my teaching career of over twelve years, I have met with countless students—of high, average, and low ability—who were not performing at the top of their game. Some of them weren't interested, some lacked motivation, some simply didn't understand the purpose of education, some struggled with complex concepts, some were just lazy and couldn't be bothered to stretch themselves, some had little or no support and encouragement from parents. One or more of these factors might be contributing to your child's underachievement, but all of them point back to parents. It is their responsibility to step in and help their children overcome these obstacles to achievement.

Your role as a parent is tri-dimensional—as teacher, role model, and mentor. As teacher, your responsibilities begin at birth and carry on to adulthood. As role model, you must live out the attributes you want your children to emulate and also exemplify your family's fundamental values. Children learn far more by observing their parents than through a set of dos and don'ts. As mentor, you must guide and encourage your child's every step forward; you must always have his or her highest interests at heart. And as mentor you are the one best placed to step in and help your child reach the greatest potential in their educational pursuits and in every other aspect of their lives. Research shows that children are most successful in school when parents are actively involved in their studies.

A parent's foremost responsibility is to raise happy, healthy, well-adjusted children who grow up to become successful adults. And, apart from their love and their most deeply held beliefs, the most important gift parents can give their children is a good education.

Education is the most powerful weapon that
you can use to change the world.
–Nelson Mandela

Education brings a broad understanding of how the world works, in addition to helping people acquire a range of specific skills. Our society holds in high regard people who have a wealth of knowledge, whether is it gained through formal or informal education. Oprah Winfrey, a great advocate of education and the prosperity and personal growth that it affords, remarks; "Education is the key to unlocking the world, a key to freedom." That freedom includes freedom from poverty, freedom from cultural restrictions, and freedom from ignorance. A good education can change the course of your child's life and open up limitless opportunities. President Obama is a classic example of how a good education can break cultural barriers imposed by race and enable a person to reach heights unattainable without it. A quality education generates upward social mobility and can help your child to live a more comfortable and fulfilled life.

My father's story illustrates the possibilities offered by a good education. He grew up in abject poverty in an African village in western Cameroon. His parents were too poor to be able to send their children to school. So my father's uncle from the city took him from the village and made him his servant at age five—nowadays, this would be termed "child labor." My dad woke up very early do the household chores before going to school. It was a squeeze for him to juggle his servant duties with his school work. He did outstandingly well in his entrance exam to the most prestigious boarding school of the time, and he won a scholarship that covered both tuition and boarding for his entire secondary and high school years. He went on to study for a degree at the only university in Cameroon and then was awarded a scholarship to further his education at a top school of administration in France. On his return to Cameroon, my father held several high-profile jobs in the government.

I am not implying that such an education is the only route to a fulfilled life. We all know of successful people who don't have any university credentials. A person can become successful in one of three ways: through educational attainment, by developing a natural skill or talent, or through entrepreneurship (creating and marketing products and services to the public). For each of these pathways, various levels of parental involvement are required.

I strongly believe in focusing first and foremost on the active support of your child's formal education, since every child is required to be in school until age eighteen in most parts of the world. Scripture admonishes, "Whatever you do, work at it with all your heart," and investing wholeheartedly in your child's education is the surest way to guarantee a good outcome. For instance, you might provide targeted support for your child in math, aimed at moving their grade from a D to a B grade for example, continuously assessing the effectiveness of your input during the term by their test results.

It's also important for parents to identify inborn talents in their children and to help develop them. American golfer Tiger Woods attributes his success in golf to the strategic guidance of his dad from a very young age. It is many parents' dream to have a child as successful in a football career as Messi or Beckham. The uncertainty is that the statistical chances of a child attaining elite level in such fields as sports and music are very slim. Research shows that at least twenty hours of quality training per week for eight years (approximately 10,000 cumulative hours) appears to be the amount of work required to reach a world-class level. That much effort takes extreme commitment on the part of the parent. Studies show that only 1 percent of those who participate in competitive sports reach the top tier. However, I definitely encourage every parent to get their children involved in a variety of extracurricular activities—that's how a child's innate talents may be discovered. I'll go into this in greater detail in Chapter 10.

The third pathway to achieving success is in entrepreneurship. Parents who own a well-established business can strategically get their children involved, training them and helping them understand how the business operates. There are many examples of long-established family businesses that have been passed on from one generation to another, for example, UK-based R J Balson & Son butchers, established in 1515, and Koch Industries in the US, established in the 1940s.

Parents can help their children develop an entrepreneurial mindset by raising their awareness of the rewards of a successful business career and teaching them the basics of financial education and the principles of wealth-creation. There is, of course, no guarantee that a child will grow up with the desire to become an entrepreneur or with the resilience it takes to establish a successful business. But I am a firm believer in giving every child a basic grounding in financial principles.

Train up a child in the way he should go: and when he is old,
he will not depart from it.
–Proverbs 22:6

This is God's divine plan for parents and children, and there's much to learn from this Scripture. It is a parent's responsibility to train their children so that they can grow up to become confident and successful individuals in every area of life—educational, psychological, emotional, spiritual, and in the acquisition of life skills.

Training a child requires, above all, an investment of *time*, because it takes time for anyone to learn a new skill and to excel at it. It takes *patience*, because the journey of success is laden with failures, mistakes, and discouragements, but with enough perseverance, parents can help their children reach the destination. One other important aspect that this Scripture highlights is training up a child in *the way he should go*. As a parent, what do you believe is the way your child should go? What vision do you have for your child? What future do you see for them? Some might argue that it's not you as a parent who should decide your child's future.

But I believe there's no mistake in this Scripture. I don't believe it is referring to a generic direction, but rather a commitment to instilling an abiding faith in your child. Where there is no vision, the people perish. Having no vision is a bit like setting out on a journey with no definite destination. Think about the days when you get up in the morning without a definite sense of purpose—such days are likely to end up being unproductive. If you don't have a plan for your child, you are less likely to invest the required time and effort in supporting them and any outcome will seem acceptable as you are more likely to accept the labels put on your child by the school and use those as an excuse for poor performance or misbehavior.

I would estimate that the way your children turn out depends 90 percent on you—how you raise them, what you expose them to, how much support you give them in their holistic development. The parents of elite athletes usually play a major role in positioning them and supporting them all along the way. That's the case with tennis legends Serena and Venus Williams, whose dad made plans that his unborn children would become tennis players. I'm not advocating that you decide what your child will become, but that you invest in making them a success in whatever they choose. I strongly believe that the outcome for a lot of children who have turned out to be dysfunctional would have been different had they been born in a warm, loving family where the parents were dedicated to investing in effective parenting.

Success in life is not a matter of chance, as the Scripture makes clear: "Do not be deceived: God is not mocked, for whatever one sows, that will he also reap" (Galatians 6:7 ESV). Raising successful children means being intentional about the outcomes, having a willingness to put in the required effort, and committing your plans to the Lord, who will honor and bless all you do.

Who are you blaming for your child's underachievement? Is it the fact that your child attends a government-run school? There are certainly flaws in the educational system, as there are in all other public sectors, but we have to make the most of the opportunities that the system offers. The school your child attends, especially if it's in a deprived area, can certainly have a negative effect on the quality of education they receive, the type of influences they are under from peers, and the motivational levels that prevail. However, with close parental support, they can still do well. Ben Carson, a gifted American neurosurgeon famous for his groundbreaking work in separating conjoined twins, was raised in extreme poverty by a single mother in a deprived part of inner-city of Detroit. With active and strategic parental involvement, children can do well regardless of their neighborhood or the school they attend.

Parents invent many reasons for not getting actively involved in their children's studies. Some assume that the school is doing enough, so they simply don't see the need to support their children. This is a faulty mindset. In a public school, there may be twenty-five to thirty students in a classroom to be taught by one teacher, and perhaps one teaching assistant in low-achieving classes. With the best intentions of helping the children to learn, how much support can one adult give thirty students who all grasp concepts at different rates? The teacher may simply not be able to give the one-on-one support that your child needs.

This is where your involvement can make the difference in keeping your child from falling behind and staying there after repeated frustration from not immediately understanding a concept. This pattern is a major reason why many students have given up trying in certain subjects and have even grown to hate them.

Some parents spend very little time at home because they work long hours to meet the financial needs of the family. This may seem like a valid excuse, but it is important for parents to plan their work schedules to ensure one parent is always available at home to give needed support to the children. For single parents, soliciting the help and support from friends and family members might be essential in ensuring the children continue to be supported and monitored in the absence of the main parent. I believe that with childbearing comes the responsibility to adequately train up a child. You alone are equipped with the love and patience needed to help a child who has been tagged with labels like "dyslexic." You are best placed to guide their career choices and impart the life skills and values they need to be successful in life.

Some parents simply lack the skills needed to support their children's studies. If this is your situation, this book is designed to equip you to support your child's academic studies so that they can achieve their full potential and go on to become successful in any area they pursue in life.

LEARN TO LEARN

A major challenge in education is *underachievement*, children failing to reach their full potential. Parents are often told during parent-teacher meetings that their children are doing well because they are reaching or working slightly above their targets. I'm not implying that if you receive such feedback your child is *necessarily* not working to their full potential. But many children are capable of doing much better than the targets set for them by their school. Although your child may have had a target set, for example, of a C grade in chemistry, there is nothing to stop them from achieving a B or an A with greater effort and parental support. If the child does get a C grade on the chemistry test, they would have met their target, but they may well have *underachieved* because they did not stretch themselves by putting in a greater effort in preparation.

Targets are set based on a pupil's prior record in assessments and a teacher's professional judgment, which is usually based on effort put into written and practical assignments, engagement in lessons, and homework. But targets are not set in stone. The more effort students put into class work and preparation for tests, the better they are likely to perform in assessments and the greater the possibility that the teacher will set new higher targets for them.

I am convinced that God has endowed every child with unique skills, talents, gifts, and abilities and with strategic parental involvement, they are capable of developing to their full potential. Children have a range of abilities—fast learners may grasp concepts immediately, while those who are not as quick may need to go over complex ideas a few more times. This doesn't mean that a slower learner cannot achieve their full potential or get top grades. Conversely, I have taught children of *all* abilities who have failed to achieve their full potential. Do you know what type of learner your child is? Is he fast or slow, or something in between? Knowing this basic factor in your child's learning ability will help you to support them better.

Some parents tend to hold very strongly to various labels put on their children that are meant to define their learning shortcomings. By doing so, such parents often fail to challenge the child sufficiently and instead seek the support mechanisms that have been put in place by the school. I'm not implying that some children don't need this extra support—they certainly do. However, it's important that parents also put in place strategic *home* support that will stretch their children.

Parents' mindset regarding their children's academic potential often determines how much effort they put in to support them. Likewise, a child's mindset, which is often determined by the fact that they have been made aware of their learning disability or difficulty, can affect their motivation to push themselves to achieve. During my years of teaching, I realized that children in high ability groups are more confident in their ability to achieve and generally put more effort into their studies. Similarly, children in low ability groups, who may or may not have behavioral issues or other learning difficulties, consider themselves "dumb" (in pupil language) and do not achieve to their maximum potential because they tend to hold on to these labels.

Your *belief* about your child's ability can provide the inner energy you need to support and encourage them to change their own beliefs about their academic potential. Flooding your home with empowering words, such as "I can," "it's possible," "you can do it," "you are a bright child," and others you may come up with, goes a long way in boosting your child's confidence and creating a mindset of "no limits." Remember that *you* are your child's most important cheerleader—don't leave it to their teachers, school, peers, or anyone else. We live in a very negative world, and as parents we need to foster a positive atmosphere within our homes.

WHY DO STUDENTS UNDERACHIEVE?

It is vital for parents to understand reasons why students underachieve to enable them to intervene appropriately. There are several factors that may contribute to a student's failure to achieve their full potential:

Lack of understanding of the value of education

A strong and compelling reason serves as a driving force in any type of initiative. I have come across students who do not understand why they have to be in school and how the subjects they study in school will help them. Students ask questions such as "How will science help me?" or "When will I ever need geography?" It is evident that students who ask such questions have not grasped the value of education.

Lack of interest

A child who is simply not interested in their studies will not put in the effort needed to achieve good results. Moreover, parents who show little interest in their children's education relay the message to them that education is not important. Parents can display a lack of interest by not supporting their children, not being concerned about poor performance, not helping them to appreciate the value of education, degrading peers who are doing well at school, or speaking in a demeaning way about teachers to them.

Lack of motivation

Motivation is the fuel that provides the energy needed to accomplish a task. An adult goes to work because they need to make money to pay the bills and meet living expenses. Similarly, children need something that will motivate their desire to achieve.

Dislike for a subject or teacher

Parents need to discuss with their children their reasons for not liking a subject or a teacher. In some cases, a student might dislike a teacher for trivial reasons, nevertheless if you feel that your child's concerns are serious, I recommend that you make an appointment to speak to your child's teacher and try to get to the bottom of the situation. It's important to let the teacher know how your child feels and about the mental blocks that may have arisen as a result. Discuss the way forward with the teacher and request that they get in touch with you about the progress of the situation.

Inadequate preparation for tests and exams

There's no doubt that academic success is the sum total of effort and ability. Students frequently underachieve due to lack of preparation for tests. Some students who lack organizational skills let work pile up and only start to study a few days before an exam. Some students have told me that they don't revise for exams, and others have admitted that they don't even know how to revise.

Lack of parental involvement

Research evidence on the impact of parental involvement on children's education shows that children are best placed to succeed in school when parents are actively involved in their education. When parents show they are interested, children interpret it to mean that their success in school must be something very important. Remember, you are your child's most important role model, and the vibes, attitudes, values, and behaviors your child sees you exhibiting will be passed on to him or her.

Low expectations of students

Students have targets set at the beginning of the school year. In many cases, these targets are not a reflection of their full potential. Teachers set targets based on data at hand and sometimes use a combination of data and the teacher's own professional judgment of the student. If a student who has a low target meets it, the school records will indicate that they've met it, and the student will be commended for it. The point I am making here is that as long as the highest level of the grading system has not been attained, there is still room for improvement. Discuss your expectations regarding studies with your children and together set some academic goals. Raise the bar and watch them rise to the challenge.

Low self-esteem

When a child doesn't believe they're capable of getting good grades, they simply won't put much energy or effort into preparing for a test. They self-defeat by anxiously focusing their thoughts on how badly they're going to perform. The obvious result is failure due to a lack of sustained study effort rather than a lack of ability. This becomes a kind of self-fulfilling prophecy.

CHARACTERISTICS OF UNDERACHIEVERS

I carried out a parent survey to learn whether parents could tell if their children were underachieving or not. Of those surveyed, 30 percent were unable to tell whether their children were underachieving, and another 40 percent were unsure, relying on school reports to inform them. Only 30 percent could tell for themselves whether their children were underachieving or not. I believe it is vital for parents to be able to determine this issue, since it is such awareness that can alert parents to step in early, before "underachievement syndrome" becomes deeply entrenched in their children's lives.

Student underachievement can have grave repercussions on future success. Children who underachieve tend to lack a sense of self-belief and to see others as better than themselves. They eventually become disempowered and shy away from trying new things and setting goals. Furthermore, they may not be able to take advantage of opportunities in life such as enrolling in a course they had envisaged or attending a leading university, because they lack the required grades or qualifications.

HERE ARE SOME CHARACTERISTICS OF UNDERACHIEVERS

Poor organization skills

They sometimes fail to take the right book with them to school or even misplace books. They sometimes forget to do their homework, hand in homework late, or simply misplace their homework assignments. Even when homework is completed, it often seems rushed, lacking in detail, and not done to the best of the student's ability.

Easily distracted

Their attention is easily drawn to other pupils' misbehavior, or they may talk a lot to other children or behave poorly in other ways. Children who underachieve tend to have poor listening skills. They usually find themselves daydreaming or looking out the window during lessons.

Poor study skills

They may be unwilling to put in the investment of time, focus, and the discipline it takes to study, and when they do actually sit down to study, they don't know how to assimilate and retain information.

Failure to take responsibility

They readily blame others and make excuses for their poor grades. They often blame the teacher for not being able to teach or attribute their failure to the subject being boring.

Misplaced priorities

They often have no real understanding of the meaning of delayed gratification. They tend to believe that having a good social life is more important than school work. They tend to admire school dropouts and those who have become successful in life without having gone very far in education, such as professional football players, inventors of computer games, rock stars, or Olympic gymnasts. Most of the time such pupils are ignorant of the effort, determination, discipline, and commitment put forth by celebrities in order to become successful.

Lack of self-belief

Because they lack confidence in their ability to achieve, they either avoid setting challenging goals, or quit as soon as they perceive that they'll lose. They tend to stay within their comfort zone, engaging only in experiences well within the realm of their strengths. Such students tend to be followers, conformist, and are often unable to voice their views.

A child's academic ability should not be their reason for underachieving. There are countless examples of people who as children were deemed to be of low ability or labeled as having various learning disorders but who went on to achieve great success in intellectually challenging careers. Here are a few examples:

Keira Knightley

Diagnosed with dyslexia at age six, *Pirates of the Caribbean* star Keira Knightley has said her struggles with reading at an early age only made her tougher. Her mother told her that she could pursue acting only if she read every day during the holidays and kept her grades up. With her dream of becoming an actress on the line, she wouldn't be stopped, and, in her own words; "I drove myself into the ground trying to get over dyslexia, and when I finished school I had the top grades." This proves that perseverance is a vital key to success.

Tim Tebow

Former University of Florida star football player Tim Tebow was diagnosed with dyslexia as a child, a condition that both his father and brother shared. In order to succeed, Tebow had to find alternate methods of learning things that others can grasp in seconds. "It has to do with finding out *how* you learn, and then you can really get it done quickly," he says. "I'm not somebody that opens a playbook and just turns and reads and reads. That doesn't do it for me." Instead, the former All-American quarterback made flashcards and memorized them over time, especially when traveling.

Delos Cosgrove, M.D.

A cardiothoracic surgeon, inventor of several medical devices, and CEO of the Cleveland Clinic, Cosgrove says; "I didn't know I was dyslexic until I was thirty-three years old. I went all the way through medical school without knowing it."

Thomas Edison

He is believed to have had dyslexia and possibly attention deficit hyperactivity disorder (ADHD). His mother took him out of school at an early age and homeschooled him. He developed a voracious appetite for reading and made major scientific breakthroughs with his unusual methodology.

My formula for academic success

SUCCESS = EFFORT + ABILITY

Achievement does not require extraordinary ability. Achievement comes from ordinary abilities applied with extraordinary persistence. Keep faith and keep up the effort, your persistence will get you there.
–Ralph Marston

HELP YOUR CHILD LEARN HOW TO LEARN

When parents understand how learning *works*, they'll be in a position to help their children make the most of learning and eventually achieve their full potential academically. Memory is the process by which what is being learned is retained. Having a good understanding of this process will help children excel in their academic studies as well as anything else they set their minds to achieve.

As soon as a concept is taught in class it is quickly transferred from immediate memory to short-term memory, where it is held for only a short period of time. But by studying or revising a topic several times, the information is transferred from short-term to long-term memory. Memory improves by repetition.

Findings of researchers at the University of California Irvine's Center for the Neurobiology of Learning and Memory suggest that when learning new things, memory and recall are strengthened by two factors: *frequency* and *recency*. The more we practice and rehearse something new and the more recently we have practiced, the easier it is for our brain to transmit these experiences efficiently and store them for ready access later. This process is called fluency.

Sometimes, parents give in to a child who complains about a topic being hard and fail to encourage them to persevere or keep trying. No doubt some concepts are more challenging than others, and a slower learner might struggle to grasp these during the lesson. I use the principle of repetition to help my children. One of my daughters, for example, struggled to grasp the concepts of long division by the "bus stop method." I used an online learning resource that showed how to work it out step by step. She grasped it very slowly on the first day, so I decided to use the same resource over a period of four days. By the last day, she became confident in doing long division. We moved from using the online resource to taking practice questions from the textbook in order to consolidate her learning. Since then, my daughter has not had any problem doing long division. The same principles apply to your child. The trick is this: if a child is struggling to grasp a concept, encourage them to spend half an hour practicing questions daily for a week, or until they get it. It should normally take less than a week for them to reach a good understanding of the concept.

HOW DOES THE BRAIN WORK?

The brain has the ability to change with learning (learning is acquiring new knowledge or skills through instruction or experience) – this is called brain plasticity. Each time a child learns a new concept or has a new experience, such as a new dance routine, it is reflected in a change in the brain: new neural pathways are created that give instructions to the body about how to perform the new activity. Similarly, failure to expose a child to new learning experiences means that no neural pathways are formed, thus weakening a child's abilities and limiting mental growth. Brain plasticity is a response to mental activity—"use it or lose it." Exposure to a new activity or learning experience creates new neural pathways and limited exposure means fewer pathways are formed.

The brain is designed to be stimulated and challenged. The problem with children nowadays is that exposure to new knowledge and experiences has been limited by technology—TV, phones, computers, video games, etc. Don't get me wrong, there are some video and computer games that can stimulate mental activity. However, because many children spend endless amounts of time in front of screens, they have limited exposure to a wide variety of other learning experiences. If the brain is not provided with appropriate stimulation or sufficiently challenged, it begins to deteriorate.

This implies that, regardless of a child's current level of brain function, their brain has the capacity to improve to one degree or another. The proven fact of brain plasticity supports my belief that every child has the capacity to do well in school—a child at the bottom of the class can improve and become average, and an average child can excel. You can help your child to improve their performance and increase brain function by encouraging them to develop a hobby, learn new skills, practice paying attention to detail, engage in physical activity for fifteen to thirty minutes daily, and maintain a healthy, low-sugar diet.

ACTION POINTS

Why is it vital for your child to achieve their full potential in their studies?

____

____

____

Do you feel your child is achieving their full potential at school? How can you tell whether or not they are?

____

____

____

List three reasons why your child might not be achieving their full potential. What do you plan to do about it?

____

____

____

____

____

Do you understand the grading system in your child's school? What is your child's target for this academic year? Do you believe your child can do better?

____

____

____

Do you know your child's academic ability (fast learner, slower learner)?

____

____

____

Do you think that all children can learn? Explain how learning works.

____

____

____

____

SET HIGH EXPECTATIONS FOR YOUR CHILD

An expectation is a firm belief that someone will achieve something. Having high expectations for your child means that you firmly believe they will achieve their full potential. I am a strong advocate for setting high and realistic expectations for children, because I believe that every child, with the right mindset and with strategic parental input, can make significant progress in learning, growing, and developing. The fact that children are of different abilities and learn in different ways should not stop a parent from raising the bar.

In a marathon, the fastest runner gets to the finish line within a short time. But slower runners who persevere and do not give up, though they may take a long time to get there, make it to the finish line in the end. A fast learner may understand concepts immediately, while a slower learner will have to go over them again and again. But it's high expectations that enable children of all learning types to achieve the best possible outcomes in their academic achievement and in all other areas of their lives. A study at the Harvard Family Research Project confirms that children for whom high expectations were set tended to perform better academically.

In all walks of life, the successful people of our time achieve their success by doing more than just the bare minimum. Professor William H. Jeynes of California State University at Long Beach revealed in a study conducted by Harvard Family Research project that parental expectations affected children's academic outcomes more than other types of parental involvement, including attendance of school events and clear rules. By setting high expectations for your child, you will be giving them something to aim for, strengthening their resilience, fostering motivation and self-belief, and boosting overall achievement. And in most cases, children will rise to the level of the expectations set for them, as long as they understand what those expectations are. Parents should have conversations with their children to make sure they understand.

Some parents are not comfortable setting high academic expectations for fear of being disappointed or out of concern that a child may become depressed and discouraged if he does not meet those expectations. Some parents don't set high expectations because they don't want to put undue pressure on their children. Some parents who may not have done well academically allow their limiting beliefs about their own academic potential to limit their expectations for their children.

Research by the Institute of education centre for research on the wider benefits of learning suggests that parents who set high expectations for their children are more likely to get involved and support their children in achieving their goals. What is your mindset about your child's intellectual ability? What is the source of this mindset? It is important that you are honest with yourself in considering the answers. How you view your child in terms of academic potential will determine the expectation you have for him. Parents who set high expectations for their children are usually those who believe that their child can meet them.

I have mentored a lot of parents who complained about their child not doing well in school. During the sessions, we would usually discuss the type and level of support given to children as well as the home structure, routines, and other factors. What usually caused a red flag during these conversations was the fact that children underachieved, in many cases, due to lack of support, adequate learning environment, structure, and routine. A negative parental mindset regarding a child's performance could be partly due to lack of involvement or ineffective involvement in their child's studies.

THREE KEY EXPECTATIONS TO SET FOR YOUR CHILD

There are three key areas that can potentially affect your child's academic performance: behavior in lessons, lack of goals, and circle of friends. Setting high expectations for your child in these areas can help them maximize their potential:

1. Behavior in lessons

It is important for parents to know how their children behave in school. Children may behave poorly in school because of peer influence, the teacher's weakness in the area of behavior management, or simply due to the dynamics of the classroom. For instance, failure by the class teacher to effectively manage student behavior might lead to a very noisy classroom that fosters an atmosphere for pupil misbehavior. Your child in such a classroom might be tempted to misbehave too, ignoring the high values you have taught them. Poor behavior in class is an important contributory factor in low academic achievement:

- It results in a waste of learning time because the teacher spends valuable class time managing behavior rather than actually teaching. If a teacher is not able to spend enough time to teach a complex topic, pupils will leave the lesson without a good understanding of it. Consequently, a pupil will either spend more time studying on their own or, in the case of many students, just give up, or moan about how the subject is difficult or about how much they hate it.

- When a pupils behave poorly in class, they lose focus and concentration. Humans are designed to focus on one thing at a time for maximum effectiveness. Therefore, it goes without saying that if your child behaves poorly in class, they will fail to understand the topic being discussed, resulting in a lack of knowledge acquisition or acquisition of knowledge in a disjointed way.

- When a pupil is disruptive, they not only prevent themselves from learning, but they also affect their peer's learning. Their constant interruption means that the teacher has to stop each time to deal with the poor behavior, depriving other pupils, who really want to learn, of quality learning.

- I encourage parents to liaise with their children's classroom teachers to find out about their children's behavior, so that they can intervene early if necessary. Here are some examples of behavior expectations you might want to consider for your child:

- Do not talk out of turn or make silly comments during lessons.

- Raise your hand to ask or answer a question, and speak respectfully and politely to your teacher and other adults within the school community.

- Avoid moving from your seat without a good reason and without permission from the teacher.

- Do not hit other children or fight with them when teased; instead, speak to the teacher about it.

- Obey classroom and school rules.

2. Set high but realistic academic goals

Goal-setting is one of the principles of success employed by top-level athletes, successful business people, and achievers in all fields.

Setting goals is the first step in turning
something invisible into the visible.
–Tony Robbins

Five benefits of setting goals

- By encouraging your child to practice setting goals, you are indirectly instilling in them one of the principles of success.

- Setting academic goals gives your child something to aim for and provides a sense of direction with respect to the grades they aspire to obtain. It also allows you and your child to measure their academic progress. Students who aim for no specific grade are usually content with achieving a grade close to the target set for them by the school.

- Setting academic goals for your child can go a long way toward helping them surpass every expectation.

- Goals help children to focus, minimize distractions, and foster better use of time.

- When children achieve the goals set for them, they feel good about themselves, their self-confidence is increased, and they are more motivated to set goals in other areas of their lives.

It is unwise for parents to assume that the educational goals set for their children at school are stretching them enough to enable them to reach their full potential. Schools set targets for children, based on prior attainment in assessments as well as the teacher's professional judgment of the child's ability in areas such as the effort put into homework, participation in class, and quality of classroom assignments. If a student has not performed well on previous tests due to poor preparation, illness, or any other reason, it does not imply that they can't do better, provided they have the parental support in place to help them. For some children these targets are a true reflection of their academic potential, but many for others, the targets do not reflect their full potential. If, for example, a child's school-set target is to achieve 50 percent in assessments, I believe that many such children are able to achieve 60 percent, 70 percent, or even higher. If there is a grade of 100 percent, why should your child settle for 50 percent? If there's opportunity to get up to a level 8, why should level 5 be acceptable for your child? If a grade of A is obtainable, why is it okay for your child to be targeted with a D grade?

I encourage every parent who aims to raise high achievers to raise the bar of achievement for their child. Children love to be challenged, especially when there's a good reward to follow. I have come across a lot of students who are just content with meeting the target set by the school when these students had the ability to do better. This, in my opinion, is a waste of potential and, unfortunately, that is the situation for a lot of children in the educational system.

Most people fail in life not because they aim too high and miss, but because they aim too low and hit.
–Les Brown

Raising the bar for your child makes room for them to stretch themselves, and with your support and encouragement, you will be surprised to find that it is achievable. It also helps to ensure that your child achieves grades at the higher end of the spectrum. For instance, if you set a target of grade 8 for your child in the GCSE class, if they don't quite get grade 8, they might get grade 7.

It's vital that you support your child in this goal-setting process. You don't want to just tell them what goals you intend to set for them, but get them to see the need for it, especially with older children. When a child understands why they need to get good grades, they will be more motivated and take ownership of their studies. It's never too early to set goals for children. It could be as simple as reading for thirty minutes uninterrupted, cutting down on mobile phone usage (though I recommend that children should not be in possession of their mobile phones during study time), or getting your active preschool child to concentrate on one task for a certain amount of time.

SET HIGH BUT REALISTIC GOALS

If your child is currently working at level 5C, for example, it might be unrealistic to expect them to achieve a level 7 by the end of term one (for some children, this could be possible with strategic parental support and the right mindset). In this case, the ideal plan might be to aim for the child to progress gradually from a 5C to possibly a 6C/6B during the course of the year, reviewing the goals every half term or end of term to ensure that they are on track for meeting their goal. The following year, I would consider progressing from a 6C/6B to a 7C/7B, as the case may be.

I encourage parents to share family goals regarding your child's studies with their teacher. By so doing, you can solicit the teacher's assessment of your child's current level and the strategies, resources, and even extra teacher input needed to help your child achieve their academic goal. It is important to not only set goals, but to walk your child through the means of achieving their goals. Goal-setting might be a new concept for them, and it is important that you patiently take them through this process and be a source of positive encouragement and support. Your child's confidence will increase as they practice setting goals and coming up with the process for achieving them.

THE THREE-STEP PROCESS FOR DESIGNING A GAME PLAN TO HELP YOUR CHILD MEET THEIR ACADEMIC GOALS

Step 1

Discuss their current attainment levels in each subject and then set new targets for the term. This target may be similar to that set by the school or may be more challenging than the school's target. Encourage your child to design a table that they can stick on the wall with targets for each subject and marks or grades obtained in assessments for each term. They should write down some reasons for wanting to meet these goals.

Step 2

Discuss foreseeable hindrances or obstacles to meeting their goals, for example, not being very organized, being easily distracted, finding certain subjects more challenging, and so on. Discuss the ways in which they can overcome these obstacles, such as seeking out a tutor, getting extra teacher input right from the beginning of the school year, considering buddy groups with bright peers, coming up with strategies to overcome distractions, etc.

Step 3

Formulate a game plan. A lot of children struggle with effective time usage. You can help your child to use time more efficiently by designing a home study timetable in which they allocate time for the entire range of things they do after school, such as extracurricular activities, homework, study, reading, playing an instrument, etc. Timetables are good in helping children with organization, and once they get into this routine, they'll find it easier to make better use of their time.

I must emphasize here that sometimes it might be impossible to stick to the timetable due to unforeseen circumstances, such as illness, attending a birthday party, or simply more homework than usual. But encourage your child to stick to the timetable as much as possible. Part of your game plan should include discussing a variety of revision and examination techniques with your child to ascertain whether they know how to study and that they understand how to obtain full marks when answering exam-style questions.

You can play an important role in ensuring that your child is revising efficiently by questioning them at the end of their revision session. You may feel that this is a bit too much, and you would rather your child became an independent learner. However, by asking your child questions at the end of their review session, you are helping them to develop the habit of reading with understanding and being able to check their comprehension. Once your child has done this exercise several times, they will acquire the ability to test their own knowledge. Habits are formed by repeatedly doing the same thing for twenty-one days. As soon as you are confident that your child has become an independent learner, you can back off.

Review the game plan with your child at the end of each term. Refer to the target sheets and grades obtained at the end of term. Commend your child for any improvements in the direction of their goal. If they didn't meet their target in a specific subject area, find out from them why they think they didn't meet their target and what they think they can do differently next term to meet it. Here are some suggested questions you can ask: Did you understand the topic? Did you understand the wording of the questions? Why did you not get full marks for a specific question? Did you study effectively for the tests? How do you feel about your revision strategies?

For a child who met their targets in the first term, I would recommend setting higher targets for the next one. Children need to be continuously challenged by raising the bar of achievement.

This helps guard against complacency, which in many cases leads to the child starting to fall back again. Discuss and come up with new strategies which could be subject-specific or general. Some revision techniques work better with some subjects than with others. In fact, your new strategies should build on issues or difficulties identified during the review process.

3. Circle of friends

"If you lie down with dogs, you will get up with fleas."

The third place for setting goals is in the area of choosing friends. I can already read the minds of some parents at this point, thinking that they would rather allow their children to choose whomever they want as friends. It's a parent's responsibility to teach their children values and life skills through regular informal conversations. By teaching your children the values and moral character to look for in a friend very early in their lives, you are shaping their thought processes and beliefs about choosing friends, and they will usually gravitate toward friends with similar ethics. Children whose parents have been sharing with them issues regarding the choice of friends and the impact of keeping the wrong type of company are more likely to choose friends with whom they share similar values and goals.

This goes for adult life as well. An adult surrounded by positive-minded friends, by friends who want to be successful, will likely end up being successful too. Likewise, an adult whose friends are negative, gossips, slanderers, who criticize others and blame others for all their problems, will do the same and will make limited progress in life.

You are the average of the five people
you spend the most time with.
–Jim Rohn

It is important to note that the issue of the type of friends your child hangs out with is a crucial factor in their academic success. This is especially true when children become teenagers, because the older children get, the less they tend to want to listen to their parents, especially so when their parents failed to develop a positive relationship with them during the childhood phase. Teenagers usually turn to friends for guidance. Therefore, it's important that your teenager's friends share your child's values and goals.

Friends can reduce your child's ability to succeed by influencing their desire to excel in assessments, to prepare for tests, and to set challenging goals for themselves, as well as negatively affecting their behavior in the classroom and their general attitude toward studies and school. If your child hangs out with friends who are well-behaved in class, respectful toward adults, and have similar values to those upheld by your family, your child will likely be the same way. There's a saying that birds of a feather flock together. If your child hangs out with children who are out on the streets till late at night and do not study for tests or do their homework, your child will very likely follow suit in order to fit into that group.

Do not be misled: "Bad company corrupts good character."
–1 Cor. 15:33 NIV

As a parent, you have your child's best interests at heart; if you don't teach them the value of surrounding themselves with positive role models and motivated, well-behaved peers, who else will? When your child is surrounded by friends who challenge themselves to reach for the stars and succeed, they will push themselves to reach for the stars too. If children are surrounded by students who have very little interest in excelling in their studies, they may find themselves comparing their grades with those of their underachieving friends and feel that they are doing very well, when in fact they are not—a bit like the one-eyed person being king in a country of the blind.

Children need to be taught that it is okay to break up an unhealthy friendship. Parents can help children spot the signs of a deteriorating friendship or one in which the friend is no longer having a positive influence over their children and encourage them to break it up. By so doing, you are laying a vital foundation for your child so that as they become a young adult, they will be able to recognize when it's time to break up an unproductive friendship.

I once had a very interesting conversation with a young lady I will call Anna, who had spent her first year in the college dorm away from home. She mentioned how she struggled to differentiate the level of involvement she should maintain with her acquaintances—her flat mates vs. her true friends. She felt obliged to hang out with her flat mates, most of whom had very different values from hers, and she gradually became influenced to do things that were outside the bounds of her values. When I asked her how prepared she felt she had been for this new experience, she honestly replied that she would have loved to have been better prepared. Fortunately for her, she came to her senses and broke friendship with her flat mates. I have mentioned Anna here to help parents understand the importance of teaching their children about choosing friends and fostering relationships that will help them achieve the high level of success they hope to attain.

Set high expectations for your children in all aspects of their lives, especially those areas that will help them maximize their academic potential. Give them something to aim for and you will be amazed to see them rise to the challenge. The world of success belongs to individuals who have developed the habit of raising the bar of expectation for themselves. Success comes through hard work, so help your children develop a strong work ethic that will help to promote them to the ranks of success. When you consistently set high expectations for your children, raising the bar will become second nature to them. The educational system may fail in this respect, so the responsibility lies with you to ensure that your children are able to reach their maximum potential.

ACTION POINTS

What is your understanding of the term "high expectation"?

____

____

Write down two reasons why you should set high expectations for your child.

____

____

____

What are the three areas of expectation that can affect your child's academic performance?

____

____

____

List three expectations you can set regarding your child's behavior.

____

____

____

Write down some realistic academic goals you would love to see your child reach, taking into consideration their present level.

Come up with some strategies that will help you to support your child.

When is it best to start speaking to your child about the qualities to look for in a friend?

What values will you encourage your child to look for in a friend?

CREATE A HOME ENVIRONMENT CONDUCIVE TO LEARNING

A home environment that is conducive to learning puts a child in a frame of mind that allows learning to happen. It is purposeful and distraction-free, allowing children to remain focused and concentrate, furthermore, it is supportive and encouraging. The nature of the home environment has the capacity to impact a child's academic performance either positively or negatively, so parents must be intentional about creating a loving, strife-free, and positive environment at home.

THREE WAYS IN WHICH AN UNLOVING AND CHAOTIC HOME ENVIRONMENT CAN ADVERSELY AFFECT A CHILD'S ACADEMIC PERFORMANCE

1. Lack of focus

A child who has just watched Mom and Dad fighting or behave unkindly to each other will have that scenario recorded in their subconscious mind, where it will be played back repeatedly. I have taught children who have come to school on the morning following a violent situation at home, and who have been very tearful, with feelings of vulnerability and difficulty concentrating on lessons. In some cases, the child has had to take time out of their classroom work to spend a good part of their school day in counseling. The result is that the child misses out on the learning taking place, falls behind, and succumbs to underachievement. A child in such circumstances will also find it difficult to concentrate at home when doing homework or studying.

2. Lack of self-esteem and self-confidence

Self-esteem is how a child feels about their worth. Self-confidence relates to a child's belief in their ability to achieve. Children with a secure sense of self-esteem and self-confidence feel good about who they are, trust themselves and their ability to make good decisions, have a strong sense of identity, are generally happier, and are better placed to achieve success in whatever they set their minds to.

Low self-esteem and self-confidence in a child can seriously affect academic achievement. Children with low self-esteem are not always eager to try new things and easily give up when challenges arise. They do not always have a positive expectation of themselves. When a child does not believe that they are capable of getting a good grade, they will not make the needed effort to prepare for tests, and so will likely fail. This tends to become a recurring self-fulfilling prophecy.

3. Lack of interest and motivation

Lack of motivation is the lack of inner drive and inner energy to accomplish. Lack of interest and motivation is a significant contributor to underachievement in school. Children growing up in a negative, chaotic, and unloving home tend not to be interested in a lot of things, especially things they deem challenging. An unloved child lacks the motivation to want to engage in even simple tasks, much less to stretch himself to tackle the more challenging ones. A child who receives no appreciation for anything they do will often lose interest in achieving anything whatsoever.

CREATING A WARM AND LOVING HOME ENVIRONMENT

It is important for parents to love their children unconditionally. Children feel secure and confident when they are assured of their parents' unwavering love for them. As parents, it is easy to assume that our children know we love them. However, it is important for parents to show their children that they love them by reminding them of it and demonstrating it in frequent pats and hugs.

When children have been disciplined, it is especially important for parents to reassure children of their love. Avoid withdrawing affection when children misbehave or do not comply with your expectations. Your child will know that you love them through the quality and quantity of time you make to talk and play with them. When the home environment is warm and loving, and parents provide appropriate support, children are able to achieve their highest potential. In such an environment, children desire to do well and to please their parents and are open to receive parental input in their studies.

NURTURING A POSITIVE AND ENCOURAGING ENVIRONMENT AT HOME

Parents can foster a positive and encouraging home environment by refraining from criticizing or blaming children for their failure or mistakes. Making children feel guilty for failure and mistakes they make is damaging to their self-confidence and sense of self-worth. Create a positive environment by being generous with positive and encouraging words. Praise children not just for massive achievements, but also for the effort and small positive steps they make in the desired direction.

Have positive expectations for your child by reassuring them regularly that you know they will do well, even when they haven't quite achieved their target. Discuss what went wrong and then reassure them you believe they have what it takes to achieve whatever they set their minds on. Children who grow up in a positive and encouraging home environment are more confident in their abilities, their ideas, and their actions. They are not afraid of making mistakes nor fazed by new experiences or challenging activities. They are self-motivated, self-reliant, and have a can-do attitude, and their expectations are high for anything take on. They take pride in excelling in their studies, knowing that they'll receive praise from their parents.

CREATING A PEACEFUL ENVIRONMENT AT HOME

Parents should endeavor to create a peaceful, positive atmosphere at home. Children think of their home as a refuge and a place of safety. A chaotic home environment that is characterized by arguments, strife, anger, and malice creates a sense of fear, insecurity, and low self-esteem in a child. Children learn a great deal about life and how to deal with various challenges by watching their parents. They hold their parents in high esteem.

Therefore, when children watch those they love and have the highest regard for tearing each other apart, it produces a sense of helplessness and confusion in their thought processes and creates warped beliefs about what family life should be like. Spouses should treat each other with love and respect in the presence of their children. Heated arguments should not take place in their presence. Children growing up in an environment devoid of peace are unhappy, they lack interest and motivation in their studies, and they find it hard to focus both at school and at home. Such children are subject to low self-esteem, they are more prone to being bullied, they may exhibit behavioral problems in school, and they are likely to join the wrong crowd.

CREATE A DISTRACTION-FREE HOME

It's your responsibility as a parent to ensure that a purposeful and distraction-free learning environment is created at home. Sources of distraction include TV, laptops, mobile phones, loud chatting, and unplanned visitors. Distractions can cause your child to easily lose focus while studying; they'll find it hard to concentrate and their ability to retain information will be affected.

All children are able to learn, but how much and how efficiently they learn can be affected by the degree of calm in the home. The environment within a woman's womb is ideally conducive to fetal development throughout the nine-month gestation period. But adverse conditions within the womb could jeopardize the child's well-being and safety and might even lead to miscarriage. Creating a peaceful home environment that is conducive to learning will enable your child to maximize their time spent studying and contribute to achieving their full potential.

ACTION POINTS

What are three ways in which a home environment that is not conducive to learning can affect your child's learning?

____

____

____

What are three ways in which you can create each of the following environments in your home?

- A warm and loving environment

____

____

____

- A positive and encouraging environment

____

____

____

- A peaceful environment

____

____

____

- A distraction-free environment

____

____

____

ESTABLISH STRUCTURE IN YOUR HOME

Children function best when their environment is structured. In homes without structure, there is no set time for anything: there's no specific meal time, children are still awake and active even late into the night, sometimes homework remains undone, household chores don't get done and may get carried over to the following day, and so on. In homes without routines, there is usually a lack of expectation and consistency from parents which could result in frequent arguments and power struggles between parents and children. Parents in such a chaotic home environment find themselves repeatedly giving children instructions and shouting at them for being uncooperative. Parents in such circumstances are at risk of experiencing stress, can easily become irritable, and may find the job of parenting to be very demanding and unenjoyable.

Having structure at home is about having a predictable routine that allows children to anticipate what happens next within the day. Routines, just like habits, are formed by repeating a pattern of activities daily. Parents can form daily routines for both school time and vacation time by talking to their children continuously about what activity comes next during the day. Creating a routine is having a plan for the day, creating a daily schedule or timetable of activities for the entire family. The range of activities to be included in the timetable will depend on the age of your children, your children's involvement in extracurricular activities, and any other family-specific engagements. A home with children of varying ages will need slightly different routines for each child. It is important, though, that main events (such as family mealtimes and clearing up after meals) happen at a specified time and involve everyone. Allocating set times for each activity can help parents to ensure that time is spent judiciously, with each member of the family doing the things they need to accomplish daily.

SIX REASONS WHY CHILDREN NEED ROUTINES

- Routines give children a sense of independence; they feel they are in control of their lives as they get into the habit of taking charge of themselves and their activities.

- Self-discipline is about a person making himself do what needs to be done without needing to be told. Creating routines involves repetition. Consequently, children develop self-discipline as they know what happens next during the day.

- A routine helps children to cooperate and reduces power struggles with parents. When children know the sequence of events during the day, they will normally just cooperate, even if they must sometimes be reminded.

- Because routines involve doing things in a set order, they help parents maintain consistency in their expectations for their children.

- Routines can help to improve children's organizational skills. A lot of adults fail to accomplish goals due to poor organizational skills. They fail to accomplish much in the twenty-four hours available for all humans. Teaching children how to create a schedule or timetable of activities for an entire week enables them to appreciate the fact that they can accomplish whatever they need to do within the time they have at hand. Good organizational skills lead to effective time management and increased productivity. Organized children become organized adults.

- Creating a routine enables you to ensure there is time for those activities that you really want to occur daily with your child, such conversation, reading, or praying together if this is your tradition. As a parent, I acknowledge the fact that anything I don't plan for is likely to be left undone.

AN EXAMPLE OF A SCHOOL-DAY ROUTINE

A school-day routine may have two parts

A morning routine of activities before the child goes to school might include "good morning" cuddles or kisses, a time of family prayer, then a shower followed by breakfast and then set off for school.

An evening routine beginning when the child returns from school might include a change of clothes for playtime, then family dinnertime, clearing up, and washing the dishes. This might be followed with ten to twenty minutes of practice on a musical instrument. Then it's homework/study time, reading a book, perhaps a bedtime snack, brushing teeth, and off to bed.

In my case, I have found a timetable useful in establishing routines for my children, given that the age gap between them is quite significant. To help create a timetable for my five-year-old daughter, we sat down and discussed the different things she thought she would most like to do, including a variety of learning and play activities as well as family dinnertime and bedtime. I wrote this out on a sheet of paper and then designed a timetable that covered every day of the week and all the activities I had noted. I got stickers and encouraged my daughter to put one into the slot for each activity she does daily.

You will find examples of some timetables I designed for my children at the end of this chapter. The timetable for my preschool daughter has a variety of activities but no specific times. The idea here is to get her to move independently from one activity to another rather than to spend a set amount of time doing one activity, since younger children have shorter attention spans. The timetables for my older daughters have timings progressing from thirty minutes for my second daughter to one hour for my older daughter in secondary school.

It's important to choose the format that works for you, either a free-flowing sequence of activities or a structured timetable. You might find this process a bit trying at the beginning if you haven't created routines for your children in the past. I encourage you to keep at it and you will be forever thankful for doing it. Dr Maltz' research on behavior change in the 1950's revealed that it takes twenty-one days of repeating an activity to form a habit. That's how long it might take for you and your children to flow into your new routine.

SIX THINGS TO CONSIDER WHEN ESTABLISHING ROUTINES

1. Family mealtimes

Family times and one-on-one bonding times are great ways for the family to connect. But due to busy and varied work patterns, it can get challenging for parents to carve out time every week for each child. Mealtimes provide tremendous opportunities for the whole family to bond together. Parents should be intentional about making family mealtimes fun and interesting, so that children will look forward to them. Families will make the most of mealtimes by turning off the TV and disengaging with all forms of distractive devices. Avoid getting into criticism, blaming, and all sorts of negative and disempowering conversations during mealtimes.

Parents can take advantage of mealtime conversations to share their life stories with their children, instill family values in an informal way, teach them about life in general, and also to get into their children's minds with the intention of subtly addressing misconceptions. Mealtimes can also be used to teach their children table manners and etiquette. In our very sophisticated world, fine details and first impressions matter; therefore, parents need to protect their children from future embarrassment that can adversely affect their self-esteem by teaching them acceptable and unacceptable behavior at the table and other aspects of life.

Depending on work patterns, parents may not both be available for family mealtimes. However, it is important for the family to have meals together, ideally around a dining table if it's available in the family home. In the absence of a dining table, the family could gather together in the same room, for example the living room or family room.

2. Homework and study

It's important for children to have a specific room or area in the home that is designated for homework and study and that is free from such distractions as TV, loud sounds from laptops, family members chatting on phones, toys, etc. Having toys within the study area for a young child can lead to lack of focus and concentration. For children who have attention-deficit problems, the presence of toys within their study area will cause them to easily lose focus, lose interest, and switch their minds off their work. Having an area designated for learning is essential, because a child's subconscious mind learns to recognize this area as a study area and switches to focus mode.

3. Extracurricular activities

When creating routines, it's important to include time for play, especially for young children, and for extracurricular activities. Play is important for a child's development because it contributes to cognitive, physical, social, and emotional well-being. While it is true that some video and computer games are mentally stimulating, I suggest setting a limit on this type of play, which can easily become addictive, and, as with TV, adversely affects the ability to focus.

Make a range of toys available, along with resources for arts and crafts, and encourage free play. If you find that your child is not very interested in toys, it might be because he finds it boring to play alone or because there's a wide age gap between siblings. In this case, I encourage *you* to make time to play with your child; this provides a good avenue to strengthen your relationship with him and also to teach about certain toys that he might not quite understand how to use. A timetable helps to set a limit for play, music practice, or extracurricular activities. Without a set time limit, children can easily spend the entire evening playing and not get involved in a variety of other activities that enhance cognitive development.

4. Screen time

TV, video games, and personal handheld devices are a great source of distraction. They can cause children to lose focus and concentration. Studies show that when children watch TV or play video games before doing their school work, it takes them slightly longer to focus their minds on their studies. Watching TV is addictive, and when children get caught up in it, it can lower the desire to read, engage with their school work, or take part in activities that can help them tap into their inner world of imagination and creativity.

Allowing your child to watch TV while doing homework or allowing TV time to eat into your child's study time will greatly impair their academic performance. Watching TV also changes the way in which a child's brain develops and can shorten the attention span, leading to attention-deficit problems. The American Academy of Pediatrics recommends that youngsters under age two not watch television and that older children watch no more than one to two hours daily of non-violent educational TV free of advertisements.

Younger children can benefit from educational programs on TV to a greater degree when parents watch with them and discuss the content. Parents can also record specific programs that their kids enjoy so they can be watched on the weekend. Take care, though, not to allow your children to spend all weekend watching TV. A 2015 study published in the *Journal of Adolescent Health* shows a link between childhood screen time and adult viewing habits: more screen time at age ten meant more screen time at age twenty.

5. Reading time

Reading is an essential skill that is strongly associated with a child's later academic success. Reading scores are one of the important indicators of academic performance. Children need to read daily for twenty to thirty minutes. Like anything else, if reading time is not designated, there will be no guarantee that your child will read every day. Parents foster the love of reading in their children when their children see *them* reading. In a subsequent chapter, I discuss strategies you can use to make the most of reading with your child.

6. Bedtime

It is important for parents to set a specific bedtime for children and to stick to it. Be ready to experience some resistance, especially if you yourself don't have a specific time for going to bed. This will also be the case for parents whose children have developed the habit of going to bed at the same time as they do, or for those whose children sleep with them. Bedtime routines are a great way to prepare your child's mind to embrace the fact that his day is coming to an end. Bedtime routines are simply a set series of activities that, when done repeatedly, help the child know it is time for sleep. An example of a bedtime routine might be a snack (perhaps a glass of milk; my children prefer cereal) followed by bath time, a bedtime story, prayer, hugs, and good nights. You can make up any routine that suits your family circumstances, but the point is that this routine will quickly become second nature for your child, making bedtime an effortless activity with fewer power struggles. Bear in mind that habits are developed by repetition. Therefore, you should be firm and consistent in getting your little angel accustomed to his bedtime routine.

National health guidelines recommend that children under five need twelve hours of sleep; older children, ten to twelve; teenagers, eight to ten. Sleep deprivation can affect a child's academic performance. This is because a sleep-deprived child goes to school feeling very groggy and grumpy and may fall asleep in class, missing out on the content covered. A child who is tired due to lack of sleep may find it hard to concentrate and pay attention. When children struggle to focus, they have trouble grasping complex concepts in lessons. Consequently, the child may have to spend more time later studying the concepts on their own. Complex concepts are best grasped in the class when taught by the teacher. Lack of sleep also affects memory by impairing a child's retention capacity, which slows down the learning process and eventually affects overall performance in assessments.

Establishing home routines not only helps *you* to live a less stressful and pressured life, but it also brings harmony in your family life and enables everyone to live more purposefully. It creates time for parents to bond, perhaps some chill-out time watching TV without the children, and opens up time for reading and personal development.

TIMETABLE TEMPLATES

	4pm-5pm	5pm-6pm	6pm-7pm	7pm-8pm	8pm-9pm	9pm-10pm
Monday						
Tuesday						
Wednesday						
Thursday						
Friday						

WEEKEND TIMETABLE

	10am-11am	11am-12pm	12pm-1pm	1pm-2pm	2pm-3pm	3pm-4pm	4pm-5pm	5pm-6pm	6pm-7pm
Saturday									
Sunday									

	Monday	Tuesday	Wednesday	Thursday	Friday	Saturday	Sunday
4.30-5.00							
5.00-5.30							
5.30-6.00							
6.00-6.30							
6.30-7.00							
7.00-7.20							
7.20-7.30							
7.30-8.00							

ACTION POINTS

Describe what it means to create structure at home.

____

____

____

In your estimation, what are the most important reasons that children need routines?

____

____

____

What are the most important activities you would want to include in your family routine?

____

____

____

Do you have a family routine? Describe in a few sentences what your family routine consists of.

____

____

If you don't have an evening routine in your home, fill in the blank template at the end of this chapter to get a head start in creating one.

INSTILL THE VALUE OF EDUCATION IN YOUR CHILD

I believe that a major contributory factor in pupil underachievement is the fact that a lot of children do not understand the value of education. In real life, adults rise up early to go to work, leaving their treasured little ones in the care of nannies, daycare providers, friends, neighbours, relatives, etc. Some adults commute long distances to a place of work they feel offers them the best reward. Others have to put up with the inhumane treatment their bosses subject them to. The principal motivating factor in each of the cases is the quest to meet personal or family financial commitments.

It isn't any different with children. They need to understand the value of education, to be able to work hard, stretch themselves beyond their comfort zone, and set challenging educational goals for themselves. Children who do not grasp the value of education do not give their best in their studies, fail to obtain good results in exams, and deprive themselves of the opportunities that show up later on in life for those with higher education.

If we want our children to value education, then we must show our appreciation for knowledge.
–Brad Sherman

One of the greatest gift parents can give to their children is to instill a desire for learning and the value of education. Learning, both self-education and formal education, is a lifelong process that is essential for achieving success in both professional and entrepreneurial pursuits. A lot of parents have relegated their duty of encouraging their children to value education to the educational system. Even with the teacher's best intentions in helping your child to value education, you have the ultimate responsibility in helping your child aspire to great things in life. Some parents struggle with the issue of instilling the love of learning in their children, because there are not many adults who actually love to learn or devote themselves to any form of learning. In today's society, technology seems to be eating into family time, depriving parents of the opportunities that family time afforded in the past to teach children family values and valuable life skills.

I strongly believe that the welfare system in socialist nations in the West, with all its merits in trying to help the poor and disadvantaged in society, gives people a sense of entitlement which says, "I am the responsibility of the state." Many families have been trapped in poverty through reliance on social welfare benefits. Children growing within such families are very likely to pick up the same mindset and probably will not value education either.

FOUR WAYS TO HELP YOUR CHILD VALUE EDUCATION

1. Model it

It is so important for parents always to remember that they are their children's most important role model. A fashion model wears outfits from new collections to allow the public to have an idea of how they look or the different ways in which they can be worn. Role models live out desired attributes, behaviors, and achievements for others to see. A fuss-free way to teach children values is by modeling them.

Your actions will speak louder than words when you live out what you want your children to emulate.

Do your children see you reading books? Do you talk to them about the books you've read? Do your children see you spending your spare time watching TV, or on your handheld devices? As a parent, you are painting a picture for your child of what happens in real adult life. Bear in mind that 90 percent of the way your child will turn out depends on you.

It's worth noting that for you to effectively model the right things to your child, you might need to do away with unproductive habits and develop new habits and values that you want to model. Your children will develop a love for learning and education when they see you engaging in various forms of learning and actually enjoying it. Help them to understand the rewards of your time spent in self-learning or formal education. It may be that you've just completed a short training that has allowed you to secure a promotion at work; it might be a personal development book that has helped you gain a specific success mindset or that has enabled you to become better at doing something.

2. Help them understand the value of getting good grades

I've taught children who didn't understand the relevance of achieving good grades, and therefore did not bother spending time in study for tests and exams. Parents should endeavor to help their children understand why they need to have good grades. Help your children to grasp that at any point in time in their lives, they are involved in an invisible competition with millions of other children their age who have been endowed with diverse gifts, talents, and abilities, and to realize how important it is for them to be on top of their game in everything they do.

Help them to understand that by achieving top grades, they put themselves in a favorable place to compete successfully for places at top colleges and universities. The average child does not understand the importance of studying at a good university. Discuss some of the benefits of studying at top schools: they will enjoy the highest quality teaching by some of the best lecturers; it will help them develop excellent work ethics; graduates from top universities are highly regarded by employers, and they have the opportunity to network with high-performing students from middle- and upper-class families, who in many cases have prestigious contacts in large companies that may open up doors to jobs.

I am by no means implying that qualifications from other colleges and universities are less valuable or that students who study in lower-ranking tertiary institutions don't get jobs. I am rather of the opinion that, where possible, parents should position their children to take advantage of the best opportunities that life affords—the best primary and secondary schools, the best colleges and universities, the best life experiences, etc. Make time to sit down with your child and look up entry requirements for their prospective courses at top colleges and universities. This will motivate your child to stretch himself and reach that high goal. Children love to be challenged, especially when they have a good reason to take on the challenge.

3. Help your child understand the value of a good education

In the introduction to this book I explained the importance of a good education. Children need to be told and shown the value of a good education. Start early, pitching the conversation at a level appropriate for your child. Have regular conversations about the value of a good education. "Seeing is believing," the adage says; show your child people in your immediate surroundings who have gone from a working-class background to abundant wealth, or people who have gone from wealth to great success by means of a good education.

Where possible, surround yourself and your children regularly with people who have been successful in their professions so as to stir up within your child a desire to study hard and get good grades. My family is blessed not only to be successful themselves, but to be surrounded by successful friends and family members. We also make it a duty once in a while to drive through middle- and upper-class neighborhoods, and even when we travel abroad, we visit affluent neighborhoods so that our children can see the lifestyles and possibilities that hard work and success afford.

As we drive through these affluent neighborhoods, we engage in conversations with our children to get them to think about why these people are able to afford such houses and lifestyles. You might be tempted to think that by so doing I am promoting a sense of materialism in my children. But my intention here is to get them to understand that through hard work, excellence, persistence, sacrifice, determination, and reliance on God, they can create the life they want for themselves. Some parents might find doing this a bit uncomfortable, but believe me, as you also see the possibilities available in life, you too will become inspired and start to dream.

4. Help your child to visualize their future

Children are generally not wired to stretch their thinking into the future unless encouraged by a parent or another adult. Lack of interest and underachievement in students are caused by lack of vision. I have taught students who even in their final year in secondary school did not have a clue about what type of courses they wanted to study in college, hence the current state of apathy in countless numbers of young people in education in our nation. Parents should encourage their children to think about different aspects of their future lives, such as the career they see themselves pursuing, the type of home they would like to have, the car they would like to drive, the quality of family life they would like to have. This is called visualization.

Visualization is about creating a mental picture of what a person wants to achieve. It is about allowing the mind to step into the future. Visualization allows your child to create success in their mind before it actually happens. Science has shown that visualization creates new neural pathways in the brain. Repeated visualization further strengthens the neural pathways in the brain, stores the images in the subconscious mind, and generates the inner energy that provides the courage needed to step into the dream.

Visualization is putting a vision on paper, calling the things that are not as though they were. You can get your child to visualize in two ways. In the first method, you can have them draft a vision statement in which they write their vision of themselves in the next ten to twenty years. Encourage them to use their imagination and creativity to describe in detail as many aspects of their lives as possible. Pay attention to self-limitations. They can then stick it on the wall and read it regularly. In the second method, your child creates a vision board by using the Internet to find pictures that reflect what they want in their future lives and making a collage which they can stick on their bedroom wall or in the kitchen or living room. I have found that children prefer this method because they enjoy using the Internet to explore images of cars, houses, vacation destinations, and so on.

The process of visualization is not cast in stone, because visions can sometimes change. When visions change, it is important to encourage your child to repeat the previous process by either writing down a vision statement or creating a vision board. The main point here is to keep your child in a constant state of inspiration and motivation.

Your role in helping your child understand the value of education is indispensable. Children who do not understand the value of education are likely to show a disinterest in it, fail to achieve their full potential, waste valuable time and opportunities that education affords, and jeopardize their future. Help your child to understand the importance of getting good grades and a good education, and save them from falling into the danger of merely going through school and gaining little value from it.

ACTION POINTS

In your opinion, what are the benefits of education?

____

____

____

Do you think your child understands the value of getting good grades and of education in general?

____

____

____

In what ways are you modeling the value of education to your child?

____

____

____

Does your child know what they want to become in the future?

____

____

____

How do you think the process of visualization can help your child understand the value of a good education?

____

____

____

Does your child hang out with friends who aspire to excel in their studies?

____

____

____

Who are the people within your community who have achieved great success through a good education and can serve as role models for your child?

____

____

____

Encourage your child to create a vision statement or vision board for themselves.

____

____

GET ACTIVELY INVOLVED IN YOUR CHILD'S EDUCATION

Extensive studies on the impact of parental involvement on pupil achievement reveal that children are best placed to succeed when parents are ACTIVELY involved in their education. You alone can exercise the greatest degree of patience in supporting your child's studies, and only you can muster the greatest determination to see your child progress from one level of achievement to another—regardless of any school report.

In my experience as a teacher, I have been rather saddened to come across parents who disengage from the responsibility of supporting their children's school work, yet still expect those children to excel academically. In this chapter, you will discover a variety of ways in which you can actively get involved in your child's studies to help them achieve their full potential.

FIVE SECRETS TO GETTING ACTIVELY INVOLVED IN YOUR CHILD'S STUDIES

Secret 1

Follow up on your child's work daily

Children learn new content at school every day. Therefore, it is imperative that each day they have a good grasp of the work covered in lessons. Otherwise, they might start to fall behind, since new concepts may be taught the next day or in the next lesson that may build upon the previous topic.

You can't assume that your child has perfectly understood the concepts taught; some topics might be too complex for them to grasp within a one-hour lesson. This doesn't mean that your child is stupid; neither does it mean that the teacher 'cannot teach', as I have overheard students say at times. The class dynamics may be such that the teacher can't teach to their full potential, because of pupil misbehavior and low-level disruption. For these reasons, make it a priority to follow up on your child's work daily, ensuring that they don't fall behind in their learning.

FIVE PRACTICAL SUGGESTIONS TO HELP YOU FOLLOW UP ON YOUR CHILD'S WORK

1. Ask about their school day every day

Ask about what they enjoyed most in school, who they played with, what they learned in each subject, and whether they understood it. Ask them to teach you what they learned—this is a powerful way of reinforcing the content in the memory. Research into how learning is re-inforced reveals that teaching others or discussing what has been learnt with others can strengthens memory. If your child struggles to teach you what they studied in the lesson, ask them to go over the topic on their own first, using all the study materials they have available, including web-based resources. If they still struggle to discuss what they learnt in the lesson, then sit down and go over the work with them if you can. You might first need to do some self-study to brush up on some of the concepts yourself.

If you are not able to help your child, then have them ask their teacher to make time to go over the work with them on a one-to-one basis. They should seek the teacher's input immediately to avoid a situation where the teacher moves on to a new concept without their understanding the previous one.

Sometimes children are reluctant to ask teachers for help. It's important that you confirm that your child has actually spoken to the teacher and that an appointment has been made for them to receive support. If you think your child is the reluctant type, you can either call the school or email the teacher directly to request help. Leave no stone unturned to ensure that your child gets the help they need in order to do well. Alternatively, you can hire a good tutor to help the child in a specific subject, if this is something your family can afford.

2. Making the most of learning in the classroom

Encourage your child to pay attention in class so that they understand the work covered. They should make sure that the teacher doesn't move on to the next topic until they understand the current content. Teach them that it is okay to ask questions in class if they don't understand. Sometimes children feel a bit shy and are reluctant to ask. This is understandable, especially in a class of fast learners. In such a circumstance, encourage your child to ask the teacher either at the end of the lesson or to make an appointment for help during a break or at the end of the school day. Encourage them to discuss schoolwork with friends as well. Sometimes peers can do a fantastic job of helping each other understand the work.

3. Good study habits

A lot of students fall behind with their learning or underachieve because they haven't developed good study habits. They not only don't know how to revise, but sometimes pile up work and start to revise only right before the test. A student who has acquired good study habits has the potential to achieve top marks in tests and exams.

- Go over work covered each day to improve understanding; revisiting concepts reinforces memory.

- Practice challenging topics every day until the child understands them. This allows information to be transferred from short-term to long-term memory.

- It is important for children to tackle school work in bite-size chunks and not let it pile up. Piling up work causes students to become overwhelmed and produces anxiety and exam stress.

- Use a range of learning styles. Our five senses—smell, touch, taste, hearing, and vision—are our learning channels. The brain stores memory coming from our senses, and different people prefer to learn through different channels. It's important that you help your child to identify their preferred learning style, since this is the way in which they most easily understand and assimilate information. Most students are comfortable using a combination of learning styles—multisensory learning, which makes remembering things easier. Neuro Science research suggest that memory is strengthened by applying a multi-sensory approach which engages all the senses in the learning process.

The learning styles are:

Visual: This student learns better by seeing and reading; for example, using pictures, diagrams, demonstrations, mind maps, posters, video clips, or flip charts.

Auditory: This student learns better by listening (to a teacher or recorded information) and by speaking; for example, telling someone else what has been learned, teaching a friend, reciting a poem, or singing a song.

Kinesthetic: This student learns better by touching, feeling, or doing things—having a hands-on experience.

• When your child has spent time studying, it is important for them to be able to test their understanding of the concepts studied. I have had students who were very frustrated with their performance on exams, claiming that they put a lot of effort into revision. It can only be assumed that these students spent time in reading but did not actually assimilate the content. You can support your child in testing their understanding by asking them questions about the work covered. You may not always be familiar with some of the content. I encourage you, in this case, to ask your child to write down questions and their answers on paper or flash cards. Or encourage them to produce visual material such as posters, mind maps, etc., which you can use to test them.

Encourage your child always to test their understanding at the end of a topic by doing practice questions. These are similar to those they would get in a real test and help them to develop better exam-taking techniques. For primary and elementary school children, it is a lot more straightforward, as there are fewer subjects and most textbooks have answers in the back; furthermore, you can print out worksheets and their answers online or purchase practice workbooks that have answers supplied.

4. Follow up on your child's progress

Encourage your child to let you know when tests are coming up so that you can support them in preparation. One thing you can do is to ask them questions from their books to test understanding. This may not be necessary if you trust your child's capacity to learn independently, but some children need close monitoring and support to achieve their full potential.

Find out what grade they obtained in a test. Help them to think about what they could have done differently to get higher marks. Encourage them to reflect on how well they studied, whether they had a good grasp of the topic, and then work with them to improve their understanding of the specific topic, or ask them to see the teacher for further clarification.

5. Extend your child's learning

Extending your child's learning is about getting your child to do more work than the school expects them to be doing. In a lot of state primary schools, children are given homework only once or twice a week, and this is not likely to stretch the child enough to bring out their full potential.

Benefits of extending your child's learning

Children are not always given homework that consolidates learning to a great enough degree. Therefore, reliance only on homework assigned by the teacher might limit your child's grasp of concepts. By extending their learning, you place your child ahead of their peers. Being ahead of peers in the understanding of concepts will cause your child's self-confidence to soar. It will also help them achieve their full potential and get better marks on quizzes and exams.

Suggestions for extending your child's learning

Get challenging textbooks in which your child can do extra work after they've covered a topic. Take care when buying textbooks to ensure that the content matches that of your child's school and testing program. You can ask the teacher to recommend books for you to use at home. Some caution is needed, though, because a teacher in a low-achieving school is likely to recommend textbooks whose content will be accessible to her students. But remember, your goal is to *stretch* your child and not to let them stay within their comfort zone. You may have to carry out a textbook search on a website such as Amazon and preview the contents of selected books to ensure that they will effectively stretch your child's learning.

There is a broad range of online resources available for children, including tests, video clips, lesson notes, and worksheets. Ensure that you have the appropriate parental controls in place when children have access to the Internet. It's very easy to get distracted and be tempted to stray off into non-educational websites; therefore, set time limits for the use of Internet-based learning resources. You can encourage your child to remain focused when doing Internet based work by engaging in a discussion with them about what they have learned.

You can extend your child's learning by getting them to do further research on some aspect of the topic they have studied. When children extend their learning beyond the scope of what they cover in school, it increases their confidence in talking about the topic at a higher level. Knowledgeable people come across as being highly intelligent.

Download past quizzes and lessons to consolidate your child's review. This will better prepare them for tests and increase their confidence in answering exam-style questions, thereby positioning them to get top grades on exams.

Secret 2

Help your child avoid distractions during study time

Sources of distraction are the television, computers, video games, music, and smartphones, on which children spend time texting, watching videos, playing games, and communicating on Facebook, Instagram, and other social media platforms. Research by Dr. Rosen, a psychology professor at California State University on the impact of studying while distracted by technology show that studying or doing homework while sitting in front of the TV, using social media or texting, makes it more difficult to learn and retain the information, increases the time it takes to complete homework, and may ultimately result in lower test scores.

I have seen students who come to school unable to focus and struggling to keep awake. Some have confessed to staying up until 3:00 a.m. watching TV or chatting with friends on social media.

Distractions are the greatest thieves of time. They hinder focus and concentration, slow down learning, and affect overall academic achievement. Imagine your child trying to study and being interrupted continually by bleeps from incoming messages or Facebook posts. How fast will they assimilate the content? Sadly, a lot of students in the educational system are underachieving from a lack of study as a result of giving in to distraction. A Cambridge university study reveals that an extra hour of screen time every day was associated with a drop of two GCSE grades, while an extra hour of homework or reading led to improved academic performance.

Don't let your child watch TV endlessly—set limits on screen time. You may adopt a no-TV policy during weekdays so that your child can focus on schoolwork. Or you may ask your child to select one educational program per day that they'd like to see. Younger children benefit more from educational TV programs when they watch with their parents and discuss the content together. For older children, set rules for the use of mobile devices, such as requiring cell phones to be kept in a specific place during study time, allowing 30 minutes to an hour for cell phone use after studying, requiring that phones be handed in to parents at bedtime, disallowing phone use during family mealtimes or family time together, etc.

Parents should help their children to wage war on distractions. The American Academy of Pediatrics recommends that youngsters under age two do not watch television at all and that older children watch only one to two hours daily of nonviolent educational television—without advertisements. On a positive note, TV and video games can be used to reward hard work and desired behavior.

Secret 3

Encourage daily reading

Reading is an essential skill that is strongly associated with a child's later academic success. Research fron the Institute of education on the effect of reading for pleasure on cognitive development over time, found that children who read for pleasure made more progress in maths, vocabulary and spelling between the ages of 10 and 16 than those who rarely read. The most successful people on earth are involved in lifelong learning by reading literature that inspires and motivates them and also enhances their personal growth and development. By encouraging your child to develop a habit of reading daily, you'll be helping them to develop one of the key habits of the most successful people.

Daily reading has tremendous benefits. Brain researchers reveal that reading improves brain function in several areas. It stimulates the formation of new neural pathways as new information is absorbed. Reading flexes those parts of the brain that deal with problem-solving, pattern-recognition, and interpretation of what others are saying to us about their feelings. It also improves memory, builds on prior learning as additional neural pathways are formed, and exercises parts of the brain that stimulate imagination. It can increase your child's IQ and help them do better academically. It can enrich language power, including vocabulary and grammatical construction. It can improve retention capacity, comprehension, logical thinking, and critical-thinking skills. Reading can help children to have better focus and concentration and, last but not least, it is a wonderful alternative to all the screens in their lives.

How to structure reading with your child

Read aloud daily to your preschool child; this fosters their love for reading and learning.

As a child learns to read, they should be encouraged to read out loud to parents. This helps to keep them interested as they develop their reading skills. Encourage your child to read with the appropriate speed and fluency, ensuring that words are pronounced properly and with expression.

Older children should be encouraged to read daily for twenty to thirty minutes. They will easily spend hours reading books they find interesting. Reading textbooks should also count as reading time. While it's likely that children will choose the path of least resistance, they will benefit more from reading books with complex grammatical constructions, since this will improve their vocabulary and language abilities.

Tips to get the most out of reading with your child

1. Include reading in your home routine. Set a specific time daily, when your child is not too tired. This will go a long way toward encouraging your child to develop a love for reading,

especially if all the other family members engage in reading during that time.

2. Read in a distraction-free environment—no TV, music, or toys. Reading is an activity that requires focus and concentration; therefore, any sources of distraction within the environment will likely cause the child to lose focus or even have their attention completely diverted from reading to other things.

3. To test retention capacity, ask the child to summarize what the story is about. Ask them questions about things that happened in the book. For example, what is the problem in the story? Who are the main characters? This strategy is important for picking up signs of learning difficulties and being able to address them at an early stage.

4. To improve logical and critical thinking, ask your child what they think will happen next. Ask about how people in the story feel in different situations and why. Ask what they would do in the same situation.

5. Ask your child to do further research on an aspect of the book that is unfamiliar to them. For example, say your child comes across the word "continent" while reading. Find out if they know what continents are. If they don't, discuss it with them, ideally using a map showing the continents. You might even get them to do some research on the continents of planet Earth. This is one way that reading can help to expand a child's general knowledge—remember that not all knowledge is acquired through formal education at school.

6. Have your child write one more chapters to continue the story, or ask them to produce a summary of the key events of the story on a cartoon strip. This can tremendously improve a child's writing skills.

7. Develop a love for reading yourself. Your child will see a reason to read when they see you reading. Family mealtimes are a great time for sharing about books that individual family members are reading.

Secret 4

Pay attention to your child's school reports

Different schools have different policies regarding the frequency of reporting children's effort, progress, and achievements. Regardless of the frequency with which you receive them, it is important to pay attention to the information provided in the reports. They are meant to give parents an important picture of their child's performance.

The information could be in the form of raw scores, standardized data, or a number or letter code. Where a number or letter code is used to indicate achievement, a key will be provided to help parents decode the information. The amount of information does vary from school to school and could include the following: a target score for your child, data representing your child's current performance, a measure of the effort your child puts into their work, and sometimes data showing the national average for children in that grade.

Reports are not meant to be used by parents to threaten or punish children. They give an indication of areas where parental input can provide leverage for the child. The idea is that there is always room for improvement; therefore, praise current effort and look out for areas needing improvement.

What information should you pay the most attention to on your child's school report?

*   It's always important to look for things that are worthy of praise to raise your child's spirits. Praise your child for meeting

their target, for good behavior, for focus and progress made. Praise your child and reinforce the fact that you believed they would do well. By so doing you are sowing seeds of positive expectations for your child.

- Behavior: Look at data indicative of your child's behavior in class. Where applicable, discuss with your child reasons why the teacher is concerned about their behavior. Help your child to develop the habit of taking responsibility for their actions by asking them how they feel about their behavior in class (this is important, because I have had instances where some students did not understand why something they did was disruptive, or why the way in which they spoke was wrong or rude).

You can help your child develop emotional intelligence by asking them how they think the teacher felt when they behaved in a certain way, how other students felt, and how they feel their behavior affects the quality of teaching and learning going on in the classroom. It is important to follow up by discussing appropriate behavior and setting daily goals with your child to monitor progress. Depending on the gravity of the behavioral problem, it might be useful to discuss your concerns and strategies for managing your child's behavior with the teacher so that you can team up to tackle the problem.

- Effort: Data on effort is meant to give parents an indication of their child's levels of enthusiasm, involvement in lessons, and completion of class work and homework. If this is an issue, discuss these aspects with your child. Get them to tell you how much *they* feel they get involved in lessons. If necessary, discuss reasons for their non-involvement (pay attention to issues such as shyness about speaking out, low self-esteem, low-level disruption that causes lack of focus, lack of interest, low-level bullying, and so on). In my experience, reasons for students' lack of effort fall into the following three categories: lack of interest, distraction or low-level disruption, and low self-esteem. Help your child to understand the benefits of maximizing their time spent in lessons. Again, when necessary, discuss any concerns you have about your child's effort with the class teacher and together, come up with strategies to help them improve.

- Progress and achievement: Data on progress shows how well your child is moving toward achieving their targets. Data on achievement in individual subjects or areas assessed indicates what your child has actually achieved on tests or assessments. In areas where your child is underachieving, ask for reasons for their underperformance in particular tests. Then ask them if they know what to do to improve next time and who they think can help them in individual subjects.

  By going through this drilling strategy repeatedly, you will be helping your child to become a self-reliant student. According to the Oxford dictionary, self-reliance means "reliance on one's own powers and resources rather than those of others." A self-reliant student is able to independently identify what went wrong, why it went wrong, and what to do to get a better outcome. Self-reliance is one of the key qualities of successful people.

- Set new goals for the following term for your child moreso in areas where improvement is required and come up with a strategy to help them improve. I firmly believe that just as intelligence and ability are not fixed, there is always room for improvement. Don't be reluctant to raise the bar for your child. Children like to be challenged, and they will usually rise up to it, especially when they have the support and encouragement of their parents. It is worth noting that sometimes targets set by the school for your child are not challenging enough to get the best out of them. There is nothing wrong with setting your own higher target for your child to help them achieve their full potential. The result will be that your child will perform *above* the school's target. Schools generally respond to such improvement in performance by moving the child to a higher ability group where a new, higher target will be set for them. Most importantly for your child, the school will recognize and celebrate their improvement by presenting them with an award during award giving ceremonies aimed at celebrating students' effort, progress and achievement.

Secret 5

Holidays can provide leverage for your child

Children always look forward to holidays and summer vacations so that they can take a break from the all hard work they put in when school is in session. They definitely deserve plenty of time to relax, play, and do other things; however, it is vital not to allow them to get disconnected from their learning. The National Summer Learning Association's website states the following: "Research spanning 100 years shows that students typically score lower on standardized tests at the end of summer vacation than they do on the same tests at the beginning of the summer." They also tend to lose study skills, and their interest and motivation to study decreases. These things can sometimes take a while to build up again. Children have a lot of time on their hands during vacations, and I personally find nothing wrong with getting them to do some school work. It's a good strategy for parents seeking to raise high achievers.

Four ways to improve your child's performance during vacations

- Help your child to identify topics they found challenging in the previous term or the previous academic year, and make a plan to go over it again until they are comfortable with it. Encourage them to use a vast range of resources for this activity, such as their exercise books, textbooks, online resources, and online video clips on the relevant topics.

- Encourage your child to improve on their test-taking techniques by having them practice answering exam-style questions. You can print out past tests from the websites of examination boards, together with marking schemes. Answering past questions will increase your child's understanding of the typical wording of exam questions, increase their confidence in answering exam-style questions, increase their speed in answering, and help them to practice answering questions fully in order to gain full marks. Self-marking their answers will help them figure out reasons for not getting full marks on long answer questions. It will also help them to have a better understanding of what examiners expect when questions are framed in a certain way.

- During vacations, you can strategically move your child forward in their learning by getting them started on topics to be covered in the next term or academic year. Getting your child to study ahead on a complex topic will help them to grasp it easily and quickly when it gets taught in school. Covering content ahead of the teacher can help children feel good about themselves and boost their confidence, especially in a subject area they tend to find challenging. It puts them ahead of their peers. Due to the complex nature of certain topics, slower learners do not always fully grasp the content in the lesson. Consequently, studying ahead will greatly benefit a slower learner. One of the habits of successful students is that they study ahead.

- Parents can extend their children's learning by getting them to carry out a Google search of aspects of topics covered in their lessons—in other words, allowing them to go beyond the scope of what their peers are doing. This can help your child to become more knowledgeable than the average child of the same age. A broad knowledge base can give them the confidence to engage in conversations on many different topics, even with older people. Not to mention that society values and respects people who are knowledgeable.

Getting actively involved in your child's studies entails following up on their school work daily, keeping up with their progress, and supporting them in overcoming distractions. Lack of, or inadequate, parental support is a significant contributory factor in children not achieving their full academic potential. Following up on your child's studies will supply the one-on-one input that teachers do not always have time to give to their students.

Every child, given the right mindset and an adequate level of support, can do well in school. Being actively involved requires an investment of time and energy, but in the end it will be well worth the effort. Investing in your child is the type of investment in which you have a measure of control over the outcome. Enjoy investing in your child's future, and I believe that God will bless your efforts.

ACTION POINTS

Write down three ways in which you will follow up on your child's work daily.

____

____

____

What advice will you give your child every morning as they set out for school, about making the most of learning in the classroom?

____

____

____

What, in your opinion, is the greatest source of distraction for your child that might affect their studies?

____

____

____

State three things you will do to limit the negative effects of distraction on your child.

____

____

____

List three benefits of reading to your child.

____

____

____

Write down how you can help your child make the most of reading.

____

____

____

What are good study habits, and how can you help your child develop them?

____

____

____

List three vital things to pay attention to on your child's report card.

____

____

____

What strategies will you put in place during school holidays and vacations to help boost your child's performance?

____

____

____

RECOGNIZE YOUR CHILD'S TEACHER AS AN INVALUABLE PIECE OF THE PUZZLE

A good rapport with your child's teacher can accelerate their educational progress. Get the teacher on your side—they are a tremendous resource to take advantage of. Teachers spend considerable time with children while they're at school and interact with them in different settings. They understand your child's strengths, weaknesses, behaviors, interests, preferred learning style, and so on. It's important for you as a parent to develop an open and positive relationship with your child's teacher so that they can feel free to discuss your child's strengths and weaknesses. You will be doing your child a disservice and failing to take advantage of this useful resource if you are not open to hearing about your child's weaknesses. Avoid being rude and confrontational; this may cause the teacher to choose not to go the extra mile with your child. This doesn't mean that you shouldn't freely express your deep concerns to the teacher.

Sometimes just a quick chat during student pick-up at the end of the school day can be effective. For an in-depth conversation, make an appointment to meet with your child's teacher—at least once a month. You do not have to wait for "parent evenings" or parent-teacher conferences, as they are sometimes called, to discuss your child's progress. Parent evenings sometimes come up well on in the academic year, and issues that should be addressed might not be discovered until then.

For children in secondary school who have several teachers, I suggest a monthly meeting with teachers on a rotating basis; or speak to your child's main teacher, requesting that specific information be collected from all teachers and emailed to you. Based on the information you get, you could plan a meeting with only those teachers who raise concerns about specific areas. Make these meetings a top priority regardless of your child's protests.

TIPS FOR MAKING THE MOST OF PARENT-TEACHER MEETINGS

For educators, parent-teacher conferences are not just another "check the box" school event. These meetings are aimed at providing valuable information about a child's effort, progress, achievement, and overall involvement and well-being within the school environment. They are not aimed at painting your child black or giving a negative report about them; therefore, be open to discussing your child's weaknesses or negative issues without taking offense. These meetings are intended to get parents engaged. Conscientious parents will use the feedback from these meetings to map out strategies they can use to get involved in their children's education.

A good way to start is by acknowledging and appreciating the teacher's effort and contribution in making your child the best student he or she can be.

Make sure you go with a notepad and take notes at these meetings. Share your family's educational goals. Some parents have set educational goals for their children based on preconceived ideas they have about their child's academic abilities. It is important to share these goals with your child's teacher. The teacher will honestly share with you what they feel your child is capable of accomplishing based on their perceived opinion of the student's effort. Be open to the teacher's opinion of your child, and focus on the reasons they put forward, because these will help you realize the amount of input you will need to get your child from their current level to the level you desire for them. A man reaps only what he sows. Therefore, your child's current level of attainment is commensurate with the effort they put in. Greater effort means better results for students. It's especially vital to find out from the teacher how you can support your child to make this dream a reality, as well as to help them discover how *they* can support your child to achieve this goal.

Discuss your child's level of concentration. Distraction and lack of focus lead to missed opportunities for learning and have the potential to cause grades to slip. You want to find out from the teacher your child's level of focus and concentration in lessons. Low-level disruptions, lack of concentration and focus, and outright misbehavior are grave contributory factors in pupil underachievement. Often, teachers will call the home to complain about a child's behavior only in severe cases. They are usually so busy planning and teaching lessons that it is impracticable to phone parents to report such things as low-level lack of focus and concentration exhibited by students. But it's important that you know how well your child is learning while at school.

Discuss your child's behavior toward the teacher and peers. Misbehavior in class affects learning, and if your child misbehaves, they are not only affecting their own learning but that of their peers. Teachers value parents who are supportive of their efforts in dealing with their children's misbehavior. I have come across parents who are very protective and defensive of their children and will believe their child's word rather than the teacher's.

You can discuss behavior management strategies with the teacher. For example, you can request to have your child moved away from distracting students or moved to the front of the classroom away from all distractions. The teacher can also help come up with strategies you can implement at home to correct your child's misbehavior at school. Maintain regular contact with the teacher to find out how your child's behavior is improving.

Find out about your child's level of involvement and motivation in class. Does your child ask or answer questions in lessons? Does he take part in group activities? Does he complete the required amount of work set in the lesson? Does he offer to help? Is homework handed in on time? Is homework completed to the highest standard? Studies on learning show that students who are more engaged during the lesson learn better, show improved academic performance, and do better on tests. Non-engagement in lessons could indicate a lack of interest in a particular subject or in studies in general if this pattern is reflected across the board. It could be a sign of resignation from trying, especially if a child finds a certain subject challenging.

Lack of involvement could also be a sign of shyness, low self-esteem, or lack of confidence. Discuss with your child's teacher the strategies they have employed to get your child more involved and engaged. Make suggestions of strategies you feel the teacher could use to improve your child's engagement. Refer to the chapter on motivating your child for success to find ways to improve your child's self-esteem.

Find out what your child's targets are for individual subjects. At the beginning of the academic year, pupils have targets set that indicate the progress they are expected to make by the end of a term or the school year. Every child in the educational system is expected to make a certain level of progress yearly. Attainment targets are set based on prior performance in assessments. In other words, how well a child performs in assessments determines their target for the subsequent term or year.

It is important for parents to know what their child's targets are so that they can support them at home and help them do better. It's worth noting, though, that targets do not necessarily give a true reflection of your child's ability; rather, they provide an indication of the amount of effort your child has put into their school work. Greater effort will yield better results in assessments, resulting in higher target being set for the pupil.

Where your child's target is below your expectations or the school's expectations, discuss with the teacher strategies and useful resources for supporting your child at home so that they can exceed their targets. Discuss your child's strengths and how you can encourage them. Find areas for improvement and intervention strategies you can use. What activities have helped your child learn better? You could even discuss these strategies with your child and ask them for suggestions on other ways you can help them to exceed their target.

Following a discussion with your child's teacher, and depending on the issues raised, you may want to request that the teacher put your child in a monitoring report. A monitoring report is a powerful tool that can be used to keep a student focused on their targets. It could be used to keep in check a student's behavior, organization, effort, and achievement over a set period of time and could be subject-specific or could cover all subject areas, depending on what the student's specific targets are.

A behavior-monitoring report has a set of targets for expected behavior. The report gets completed by the class teacher to reflect the student's behavior in class. At the end of the school day or at some point during the school day, the student reports to the teacher who is in charge of following their progress, and together they have a conversation about the student's progress toward meeting their targets.

It is important that the student's parent discusses their child's progress daily while they're on monitoring report. In my experience as an educator, I can affirm that monitoring reports have proven to be very effective in bringing about a turnaround in pupil behavior. As a parent, you may not only request that your child be put on monitoring report, you can also recommend specific targets for your child.

Some parents consider monitoring reports to be negative, thinking that the student might be seen by their peers as not being good enough. It is important that you discuss with your child your reasons for wanting them to be placed on monitoring report, and how it is going to benefit them. Encourage your child to focus on the end result, reassuring them that it doesn't matter what others think about them. Once you are able to carry your child along, they will go through it effortlessly and more successfully.

Keep communication going with the teacher so that you remain abreast of your child's progress. It's important that your child not be on this report permanently; generally two to four weeks is enough time to start to see changes in a child. Remember, whatever it takes for you to support your child in becoming a high achiever, go ahead and do it. Ask the teacher to keep you informed about your child's progress or challenges that arise before the next meeting. Don't forget to revisit topics brought up at the last meeting as this will help you evaluate the progress your child is making.

After each meeting, make time to talk to your child so you can address issues and come up with solutions. Blaming, scolding, or punishing is counterproductive and causes your child to put on a defensive cloak, close up, and begin to resent the teacher. Discuss the issues arising within a fun family setting. It's always a good idea to start with strengths, lavish praise, and reward your child with something they appreciate, possibly an outing to their favorite restaurant or fun activity. When discussing areas for improvement, help your child to come up with some solutions of their own to any issues that have arisen; this technique helps children to become self-reliant. Come up with a time frame within which you can both expect to see improvements, for example, you could review targets weekly, bi-monthly, monthly, every half-term, or even every term, depending on what the areas for improvement are.

Maintain a good relationship with your child's teacher and take maximum advantage of their knowledge, skill, and expertise to ensure that your child makes the most of their time in school and achieves their full potential.

ACTION POINTS

Write down three reasons why your child's teacher is paramount in helping them achieve their maximum potential in their studies.

____

____

____

How often do you intend to contact your child's teacher regarding school work?

____

____

____

Write down some questions you can ask the teacher that will give you a good idea of your child's behavior in class.

____

____

Write down some questions you can ask the teacher about your child's level of engagement in lessons.

____

____

____

What questions can you ask the teacher to ascertain whether your child is achieving their full potential?

____

____

____

What strategies will you put in place that will help you move your child ahead in any problem areas you have identified?

____

____

____

USE THE POWER OF MOTIVATION TO UNLEASH THE GENIUS IN YOUR CHILD

Motivation is the fuel that powers the accomplishment of goals; it can empower your child to do their best all the time. It has the power to quash every negative and limiting belief that has been planted in your child's mind. It has the potential to raise your child's self-esteem and to help them overcome any struggles they may face in maintaining a strong sense of identity. All humans thrive better in an atmosphere of encouragement and positivity—motivated employees will seek to perform to the best of their ability, and motivated athletes stretch themselves for top performance.

Parents should endeavor to motivate their children, realizing that they are the ones who have their children's best interests at heart—more so than educators, the government, or any other person who may have a direct or indirect interest in them. Parents are best placed to motivate, inspire, and encourage their children to do well in school and in everything else that they need to accomplish.

We and our children are continuously bombarded by all forms of negativity, whether self-inflicted or emanating from external sources. Negativity disempowers, discourages, lowers self-confidence, and produces a mindset of failure in adults and children alike. Some sources of negativity in your child's life are:

Negative self-talk; for example, a child receives a poor score on a test and says to himself, "I'm a failure, I'm stupid," or a child looks at a challenging task and says, "I can't do it, it's hard."

The media; there's negativity in many TV programs and movies that children watch and in the books they read.

Adults in a child's life; children receive negative input from adults they come in contact with. It may range from teachers communicating discouraging messages to our children, such as 'you can't study this course because you don't have the ability to do so" to parents who sometimes throw disempowering words at their children that can crush their sense of self-worth.

It's a pity that in today's world most people find it easier to say negative things. That makes it more important than ever to surround your child with positive and encouraging words that prompt them to focus on possibilities and solutions to challenging situations and help them to develop a "can do" outlook.

FIVE WAYS TO MOTIVATE YOUR CHILD TO DO WELL IN SCHOOL

1. Show interest in your child's school work

Showing that you are interested in your child's studies encourages them to pay more attention to their studies and to seek to do their best. When children know that their parents are genuinely interested in their schoolwork, they get the message that their studies are important. Children generally love to please their parents and will try hard to please them in the areas they know their parents have a keen interest in.

You can show interest in your child's schoolwork by asking them what they learned, whether they understood the work covered, and what they found interesting. Get into discussions about the subjects covered in school, show some excitement about the topics, and, where possible, find real-life scenarios where the concepts apply and talk about them. Through regular conversations with your child, you can also find out when they will be having tests or exams. Get involved in the test-preparation process to ensure they study adequately, and find out what scores they receive on tests. Providing such hands-on support speaks louder to your child than your words about how much interest you have in their studies and about your desire for them to do well.

2. Have positive expectations for your child

Having positive expectations for your child might be expressed as, "I'm sure you will do well," or "I trust you are more than capable of doing it." As children grow up, they have a better understanding of what their parents expect of them through their conversations and interactions.

By having positive expectations for your child, you are indirectly raising the bar in all areas of his life. This information usually gets stored within a child's subconscious mind and produces expected results. Parents who have positive expectations for their children raise happy and self-confident children. For example, Anna gets in trouble in school for failing to do homework, and if Anna's dad has positive expectations for her, he might say to her, "Anna you are always good at completing and handing in your homework by the deadline; what do you think happened on this occasion?" This question will lead Anna and her dad into a conversation about the reasons Anna did not do her homework and how he can support her moving forward so that she doesn't find herself in this situation again. This way of handling the problem emphasizes her dad's expectations of her. Children do not like to disappoint their parents, especially when parents have high expectations of them.

3. Support your child in learning from their mistakes

It is essential for parents to change their notion that failure is only bad. Making mistakes and failing create immense opportunities for learning and self-improvement. No one has ever achieved great success without failure in the process.

Children who are afraid to fail avoid trying new things, are reluctant to take leadership roles in school and, generally, avoid stepping out of their comfort zone. In the example mentioned above, the conversation between Anna and her dad helped Anna to realize that it is okay to make mistakes or fail at something, provided we learn lessons that will help us do better in the future.

Parents should bear in mind that the way they handle situations in which their children make mistakes or fail to accomplish what was expected of them can affect their responses. When parents shout at children and punish them for making mistakes (unless in a situation where the mistake or failure is a direct result of outright disobedience), it creates in their children a fear of making mistakes, a fear of trying new things, and may possibly lead to lying to cover up mistakes or failure. The child may also feel a sense of insecurity, because they don't perceive their parents as able to provide the covering they so desperately need in times of weakness. When children make mistakes, it is okay to express your dissatisfaction with their performance, but, after discussing lessons learned from their mistakes, it is also important, in order to avoid damaging their self-esteem, to reassure them of your trust in them and that you believe in their ability to do better.

4. Praise your child regularly

It is important for parents to understand that the words and tone of voice they use when speaking to their children are able to build up, empower, and motivate them. On the other hand, they can also damage their self-esteem, sense of empowerment, and motivation. You cannot over-praise your child; therefore, don't withhold praise or encouraging, positive words. Praise has the power to generate positive energy within a person that provides the drive to want to do well.

Adults, too, are motivated to do better when praised or appreciated for doing well. Women love it when their husbands express appreciation often—it might be their hairstyle, how good they look, how delicious the food is, etc. A woman whose husband appreciates her food will want to come up with more delicious meals for him. A man who is appreciated for the effort he puts into housework or for being a good father or for adequately providing for the family will be motivated to want to do more. A child who is appreciated for doing household chores or for being polite will seek to do more to please parents.

Praise works miracles for everyone, and it's a powerful tool parents can use to motivate their children to do well in school. Children want to please their parents, especially when they know that they'll be commended. Praise can also boost your child's self-esteem and increase their overall state of happiness and contentment. Be specific as you praise your child; it helps them to acknowledge and celebrate their demonstrated strengths and accomplishments. Some children find it hard to acknowledge the things they are good at, often viewing their peers as being better than themselves. Praise both the small efforts and the big achievements. Tell them and show them how proud you are of their efforts. Children feel good about themselves when parents share their accomplishments with friends and family members. Use encouraging words to keep them going when they are faced with a challenging task—tell them you know they can do it, tell them you believe in them, remind them of their previous achievements.

5. Reward effort and achievement

Rewards are a great motivation for achieving success. Everyone likes to be rewarded for their efforts, and actions that are rewarded are likely to be repeated. When children know that their parents or family members will reward them for making progress in their studies, they will work hard to earn it. It is important to not only reward children for massive achievements but for the little efforts they put in here and there. This helps the child to understand that great things can be accomplished through small positive steps. If your child is currently achieving grade D for example in his tests, and you want to see him to progress to a B or A within one academic year, it's important that you reward him when he gets a C. That will stir him to keep working hard toward his goal.

Rewards do not have to be expensive technological gadgets or activities; children can sometimes be easy to please and tend to appreciate gifts that parents may consider small. Rewards for very young children might be a sticker for saying "please" and "thank you," a chocolate bar at the end of the school day for completing their work in class, a video game time for studying hard, a trip to the movies or a restaurant, or a wished-for toy. Older children will appreciate money to buy their favorite outfit or sneakers, some one-on-one time with a parent at a favorite spot of their choice, or going out with friends during the weekend. The list is immense, and I suggest that parents use their creativity in coming up with rewards that are commensurate with the effort or achievement.

Your child is loaded with treasures and abilities that do not always manifest themselves fully. Children are different—some are self-motivated and will challenge themselves to give their best in whatever they are involved in; others need encouragement and motivation to give their best. Know your child, avoid comparisons with other children, and do everything you can to support, encourage, and motivate them to achieve their maximum potential in whatever they do.

ACTION POINTS

"We live in a negative world." What is your understanding of this statement?

____

____

____

What are some of the sources of negativity that bombard your child every day?

____

____

____

Why are you the best source of motivation for your child?

____

____

____

Write down three ways in which you can show interest in your child's studies.

____

____

What does it mean to have positive expectations for your child?

____

____

____

Write down some statements you can use to communicate your positive expectations to your child.

____

____

____

Describe how you can help your child learn from mistakes or failure.

____

____

____

9

CULTIVATE A HEALTHY RELATIONSHIP WITH YOUR CHILD

Great relationships of any sort do not just happen. There are vital ingredients that together contribute to the development of a great relationship, including love, care, making time to interact together, and good communication. Parents need to be intentional about nurturing a positive relationship with their children. You are your child's first teacher and most important role model and mentor.

A teacher tells or shows a student what to do. A role model lives out or exemplifies the desired attributes or behavior they want a person to emulate. A mentor both teaches and lives out the teaching, and then follows up on the mentee to ensure that the desired attributes and behaviors are formed in them.

Parents have a hefty role to play in their children's lives, and one of the most important ways they can influence their children is by cultivating a positive and productive relationship with them. Such a relationship within the family is characterized by love, trust, abundant encouragement, support, and a sense of security. A positive relationship between parents and children becomes more crucial when children become teenagers, since teenagers tend to listen less to their parents as they seek to become more independent.

BENEFITS OF DEVELOPING A POSITIVE RELATIONSHIP WITH YOUR CHILDREN

- It helps parents in instilling values and life skills in their children.

- It helps parents exercise their responsibility of guiding and supporting their children in making crucial choices and decisions in life.

- It builds trust. In families where the relationship between parents and children is strained or nonexistent, the children may struggle to trust their parents enough to open up to them about anything. It is better for your child to open up to you than to peers or other adults who might not share your values and who do not have your child's best interests at heart.

- It helps parents raise happy and confident children who grow up fully equipped with everything they need to create a great life for themselves.

- It offers a hassle-free way of teaching children values, and of setting expectations and boundaries within the home.

- It allows parents to be the greatest influence on their children, protecting them from the negative external influences of friends, the media, warped values, mixed messages, and everything else out there. Teenagers are easily influenced by friends whose values might conflict with those of your family. Be the most important voice in your child's life. Children who have a good relationship with their parents tend to be open to discussing any topic and are also more receptive to considering their parents' ideas and opinions.

BARRIERS TO PARENTS CULTIVATING A POSITIVE AND PRODUCTIVE RELATIONSHIP WITH THEIR CHILDREN

Building successful relationships of any sort requires intentionality, a commitment of time, and prioritizing the relationship above anything else.

Five things that hinder parents from cultivating a positive relationship with their children:

- Parents' lack of understanding of the need to spend time with children. Some parents simply do not see the need to maintain a relationship with their children. In some cases, culture plays a role in the limited interactions between parents and their children. In a lot of cases, parents tend to raise their children in a way similar to the manner in which they were brought up. Some people grew up in certain parts of the world where it was standard for parents to have limited interactions with children. Such people are uncomfortable interacting naturally with their children.

- Lack of time: Some parents don't plan time to interact with their children. A child perceives a parent's love by the amount of time they spend with them. In all areas of life, people invest time in the things that matter to them. If parents want to make family a priority, they need to include *time* for family in their programs and commit to it. I once heard a speaker recommend that parents spend *quality* time at work and *quantity* time at home, and I felt it made sense, because by spending a lot of time with your children, you get to connect more intimately with them, strengthening love and trust. Blocking out some quality time, maybe once a week or once a month, is more productive for one-on-one bonding time with each child.

Parents will get the most from interacting with their children informally when there's no time restriction.

- Work: Some parents work long hours, have more than one job, or are very much involved in running their businesses. At the end of the day when they return home, they are very tired and too overly stressed to want to engage with their children and spouses. While parents need to work to be able to meet their financial demands, it's important for spouses to strike a better balance between work and life, so that family does not suffer. In some families, children spend most of their day with nannies or at daycare. Spouses should where possible arrange their work schedules in such a way that one parent is always available to be with the children. Time not spent with your children cannot be regained. Time flies, and before you know it, your children will be grown up and ready to leave home for college—flying with their own wings.

- Poor parenting style can greatly affect the relationship between parent and children and create constant friction, anger, and resentment, until a gorge eventually develops. Parents who struggle with effective and positive parenting strategies should seek advice and help from organizations that focus on educating parents to help them acquire better parenting skills. Lots of books have been written to equip parents with the tools needed to be effective parents; there's also a lot of information on parenting that can be found through Google. I like this quote from Henry Ford: "Anyone who stops learning is old, whether at twenty or eighty. Anyone who keeps learning stays young. The greatest thing in life is to keep your mind young." Parents should be open to educating themselves in any area of their lives in which they feel they are deficient. Self-education and lifelong learning are key to being successful in anything in life.

- Distractions: In today's world, adults and children alike fall prey to distractions. The greatest sources of distraction are TV, smartphones connecting people to the external world twenty-four hours a day, personal laptops, tablets, and so on. Technology seems to be taking over entire families. Parents and children alike are on their personal devices, checking every message that chimes in around the clock, watching movies, listening to music, playing games, chatting with invisible friends on social media, all to the detriment of time spent with family.

Before the advent of this wide range of technology, families used to sit together within a communal area like the living room and interact together in various ways. The result was solid and close-knit families in which parents could effectively instill their values and beliefs in their children. Parents who value family time make it their duty to set rules at home to control the amount of time members of the family spend on technology. Some families have set times when all members of the family sit together in the same communal room and interact without any distractions from technology, permit no TV or phones during mealtimes, do household chores together, and so on. Family dynamics vary, and therefore parents should come up with rules that work for their specific realities.

TIPS FOR BUILDING A POSITIVE RELATIONSHIP WITH YOUR CHILD

1. Talk with your child

Parents should make use of every available opportunity to talk to their children. You can talk to them at mealtimes, when doing household chores together, or while riding in the car. Keeping conversations going on a continuing basis with your child will help you to know them better. You'll know how they think and feel about different things, and, most especially, you can share your family values and set clear boundaries and expected behavior with them in an informal way.

By making time to talk to your child, you can take advantage of teachable moments to impart life skills, correct their misconceptions about various issues, and help them understand how things work in real adult life. You can talk about anything and everything, taking care to deal with sensitive issues in an age-appropriate manner. Never shut down questions your child raises. In some cases, you might need to speak with friends to get their advice on how they handled certain issues or search your concerns on Google (taking care to rely on wisdom from God, since there's such a mix of constructive and destructive ideas and opinions on the Internet).

Children enjoy their parents giving them their undivided attention. Try not to talk to your child while watching your favorite football team or movie or while interacting with your smartphone. Show that you value your child by stopping every activity and focusing solely on them. If you don't feel it's the right time to interact with your child, tell them nicely that you would rather have this conversation at a specified later time (obviously, not a time too far off, since they might forget what they intended to share with you!).

2. Interact with your child

Parents should make time to relate with their children in a variety of ways and settings, such as playing and having fun at home, in public parks, at theme parks, etc. Parents can also relate to their children when doing household chores together, such as cooking, gardening, or cleaning the house. Other opportunities for interacting are going for a walk, going to the gym with your teenager, going fishing, family sporting activities, family bonding time, one-on-one bonding time with individual children, and family worship times.

Family bonding time is time set aside weekly, biweekly, or monthly for all members of the family to come together for more meaningful conversations, such as setting academic goals, teaching important life principles, planning family activities, or discussing solutions to issues that arise. It's not a time when children just sit and listen, it's important for parents to get their children involved in these discussions. This allows all family members to contribute to issues relating to the family and feel a sense of belonging.

One-on-one bonding time is protected time during which one parent (or both) interacts with one child at a time. It is that special thirty-minute or one-hour slot during which parents give undivided attention to just one child. It allows for close bonding between parent and child and fosters love and trust. It's a time for your child to talk about anything, from complaining about things going on at home that they might not be happy with to discussing their interests, friendships, and anything else they might want to talk about. It is also a great time to mend broken bridges, especially when there has been a breakdown in communication between parents and a teenage child.

During this time, it is vital that you listen to your child, avoiding a judgmental or critical attitude, and try to understand them and use wisdom to deal with issues that arise. Have lots of fun, joke, and laugh with your child—make this a memorable time and they will always look forward to it. It's ideal to fit this time into the family routine to ensure that it actually happens. Parents can sometimes get caught up with such a multitude of activities that those that haven't been scheduled might be forgotten. Making time for your child communicates to them the value that you place on them.

Family worship time provides an avenue for parents and children to bond as they learn the precepts of their faith and pray together. It is a time of submission to the greater authority of the Scriptures and for each member of the family to express their humility before God and each other. It's a great time to instill faith in your children, a great time to share family values and goals. It's a time to share personal needs and family challenges and to pray for them. Family worship, just like any other activity that can foster family unity and happiness, should be prioritized and planned for, so that children perceive the value you place on important things by ensuring that they happen through a structured home life.

Interacting with your children in an informal setting allows the family to bond and creates a sense of trust, openness, and security in your children. This helps them to feel free to talk to you about anything without fear of being judged or criticized, allowing them to take advantage of the support mechanisms that family affords. Make time to attend your children's school and extracurricular performances, since children always look for their parents in the crowd and are eager to do their best to impress them.

3. Make your child feel important

Children look up to their parents for validation. Sometimes the manner and tone of voice that parents use when speaking to their children can belittle them and make them feel worthless or that their opinions do not count. You can make your child feel important by speaking to them as mature and intelligent individuals. Some parents shout and scream at children indiscriminately, which can make them repressed and cause them to withdraw and become uncommunicative. This point is more important as children go through the teenage years.

In conversations with your children, ask for their opinions when you deem it advisable and in matters that affect them. Acknowledge good suggestions they make; this helps children understand that their thoughts and ideas make sense and are valuable. In situations where you think your children's opinions do not quite make sense, avoid being negative and rather use wise and positive words to get them to think in line with your ideas. By so doing, you will be preserving their self-esteem.

As a teacher, it's easy to spot a confident child who has raised in a home environment where they freely express their opinion. Such children believe in their ideas even when controversial, and are free to express their views without fear of what others will think of them. During group work, such children quickly take on a lead role and direct how things should be done. Less confident children tend to be followers and sometimes put up with things they do not necessarily agree with. Less confident children can also succumb to bullying. Help your child to become a leader by treating them with respect, valuing their opinion, and getting them involved in certain aspects of decision-making, such as where to go for a meal, where to go on a family day out, or what activities to engage in during vacations.

4. Use positive discipline

Discipline is an important part of parenting; it helps children to do the right things. Discipline, therefore, is everything a parent does to help their children to do the right things—teaching, guiding, and directing. The Scriptures tell us to train up a child in the way he should go, and when he grows up, he will not depart from it. Discipline helps children to understand the value of rules, and that in real life, nations have specific rules that are put in place to maintain peace and order. Parents who do not discipline their children are indirectly raising law breakers who will eventually violate rules in school and within the community. It is important for parents to convey the importance of discipline to their children and most especially remind them continually of the love they have for them. Discipline is not meant to damage a child physically or emotionally, but to help them learn lessons and become better.

Inappropriate use of discipline can sometimes cause a breakdown in the relationship between children and parents, more so with teenagers. Using harsh methods of discipline can lower self-esteem and cause children to become angry, resentful, withdrawn, or rebellious, or even to develop a hatred for their parents. When the relationship between parent and child breaks down, the child may close up and become unreceptive to any parental input.

THREE STEPS TO POSITIVE DISCIPLINE

Step 1

Set clear boundaries and expectations

Parents need to establish clear rules, expectations, and boundaries in the home and ensure that children have a clear understanding of what they are. It might be useful to put up a poster with the set of rules, just to make sure the children grasp it. It is not uncommon for children to claim that they were not aware of the rules.

Step 2

Establish defined consequences

Parents should make their children aware of the consequences associated with not following rules within the home. The consequences should be commensurate with the offense. There is a wide variety of age-appropriate methods of discipline, such as a time-out, deduction of privileges and allowances, assigning chores, withdrawing favorite toys or cell phones, and so on.

It's crucial that the consequences you choose actually cause your child to learn the necessary lessons. It is also important to choose consequences that you will actually follow through on. Threatening a child for example with not going on a family holiday that has already been paid for is not realistic unless the parent is willing to lose the money they have paid for it. When parents do not follow through on the consequences they have established, their children may very well come to believe that they may not follow through on other consequences in the future. The result might be further misbehavior and lack of cooperation, and eventually the parents may lose all authority over the child.

Step 3

Reconnect

Following the carrying out of the consequences, it's important to reconnect with your child to help them learn the appropriate lessons and to reassure them of your love. This is the time to encourage your child to reflect on their behavior, apologize to you or any other member of the family as appropriate, and then receive reassurance that you love them despite hating the behavior, followed by hugs and kisses. This is a powerful way of raising a child's spirits while at the same time helping them to learn to take responsibility for their disobedience and learn lessons from the situation.

Positive reinforcement focuses on using rewards to get your child to act or behave in the way you want them to. It is a very efficient way to alter behavior. Consider the following scenario: John's challenge is poor behavior toward peers and adults in school, and he has been in trouble daily for the past few weeks. There's a choice of two approaches to handling this situation. You could apply a consequence each time he fails to meet the required expectation, or you could come up with a reward system that will elicit the desired behavior. You could give John a candy at the end of each school day when he has been well-behaved, or you could come up with a star chart on which you stick a star for each day he has been well-behaved, and at the end of the week offer him a more significant reward. Positive reinforcement works best for behaviors that might need more time to get your child to change, such as in forming new habits that will help improve behavior. Discipline is a gray area in which, in many cases, one size does not fit all. Children have different personalities and respond differently to different forms of discipline. Parents should try to understand their children and pray for wisdom in handling various situations.

A positive and effective disciplinary strategy will not only help to strengthen your relationship with your child, but will also ensure that he learns life lessons and skills, acquires vital values, and comes to understand that discipline and respect for authority are crucial to becoming a law-abiding citizen.

ACTION POINTS

What are the vital ingredients that are key to building healthy relationships?

____

____

____

What are some of the barriers parents face in developing a positive relationship with their children?

____

____

____

List three benefits of developing a healthy relationship with your child.

____

____

____

Describe the actions you will take to further nurture your relationship with your child.

____

____

Formulate some rules you will put in place in your home to ensure that distractions do not eat up time you could spend interacting with your child.

____

____

____

How can you make your child feel valued?

____

____

____

Write down the three steps to positive discipline.

____

____

____

How does positive reinforcement work?

____

134

____

____

ENCOURAGE EXTRACURRICULAR INVOLVEMENT

Extracurricular activities encompass all non-academic activities that your child can become involved in, either in or outside of school, ranging from sports, music, drama, arts, and crafts to volunteering and hobbies. Extracurricular activities also include participation in clubs, such as chess, skateboarding, debating, or writing, as well as involvement in church pursuits. They can help your child become well rounded. A well-rounded child is one who is skilled, capable, or knowledgeable in a number of areas; does well in school, plays sports, and has a variety of experiences. Raising a well-rounded child requires consistency, dedication, and patience on the part of the parents.

Extracurricular activities are fun and enrich a child's range of experiences. They let children disengage from schoolwork and help them develop useful life skills while doing something they enjoy. Extracurricular activities help children to discover themselves and also provide a social outlet where they can meet new people and make friends, in many cases lifelong friends, who help them maintain a healthy balance between work and play.

Such activities can reveal your child's unique gifts, which can be pursued and developed into sources of great satisfaction in adult life. In some cases, a strong passion for an extracurricular activity can guide a choice of career. A person's life purpose is generally linked to what they enjoy doing, what they excel at, what they are passionate about, and what they love to share with others. It's possible for children's hidden gifts to go undiscovered and undeveloped if parents do not encourage them to get involved in a variety of activities.

Parents should be careful not to allow too many extracurricular activities to interfere with their children's studies. Taking part in several activities can lead to inefficiency—your child may struggle to perform at the top of their game in every one of them, not performing as well as they might have if they had focused on fewer—a jack of all trades and master of none. That can eventually breed discouragement and low self-esteem, especially if friends are doing well and progressing in leaps and bounds and receiving awards in activities they are involved in.

Involvement in too many extracurricular activities can be time-consuming and exhausting for a child. This can result in the child not having enough time to focus on their school work, or coming to their school work feeling too exhausted to focus and assimilate the work. If you find yourself in a situation where your child is currently involved in several extracurricular activities, it's vital to help them understand the need to focus on just a couple of them so as to maintain the correct balance with their school work.

It's also important that *you* not make the decision on which activities your child participates in, since extracurricular activities are really about what your child enjoys doing. When your child chooses an activity they enjoy doing, they're likely to be motivated to do their best, they'll tend to practice more, and they may well gain recognition for good performance that will help to boost their self-esteem. It's not uncommon for parents to try to impose an activity they want their child to pursue, thereby killing the sense of joy, fulfillment, and happiness the child could derive from an activity they are really passionate about.

Two out-of-school activities are recommended, perhaps a sport and a musical instrument. Also encourage your child to take advantage of school-based activities and clubs that meet during the school day and are unlikely to affect how much time they have left for studies in the evening

BENEFITS OF EXTRACURRICULAR ACTIVITIES

Extracurricular activities can help children learn new skills and discover their unique talents. God has created humans with a great deal of potential, but many people go through life never discovering their gifts, talents, and abilities. Parents can help their children to learn new skills and develop their unique talents and gifts by encouraging them to try out new things at school and exposing them to activities and experiences outside of school at an early age.

As your child begins to participate, you'll soon discover which activities they show a strong interest in, and they will benefit most from focusing their passion and energy on one activity and excelling in it. By doing so in the case of a sport, for example, it will be easier for your child to develop their skills faster, and possibly to a top level. Who knows where this skill or talent may lead?

Many successful people achieved success by turning their passions into a money-generating venture. A classic example of how passion and dedication to improving a skill can lead to massive success is Bill Gates, the richest entrepreneur on the planet, founder of Microsoft, the company that created Windows software. Bill Gates developed an interest in computer programming at age thirteen, and was very fortunate to have had unrestricted access to a computer. He had a passionate desire for programming and was committed to learning how to do it, spending hours on the computer to master it.

The biographies of star legends Venus and Serena Williams testify to the effects of dedicated parental involvement in nurturing children's gifts. They also show the importance of focusing on one activity and committing to regular practice. Their father Richard had envisioned the sisters' path into professional tennis even before they were born. Richard enjoyed watching tennis on TV and dreamed he would one day see his yet-to-be-born children playing tennis on TV. He used the information he had learned from reading tennis books and videos to instruct his daughters in various aspects of the game. He started training them very early and would have them practice six hours a day, playing with tatty rackets and dud balls against a wall or on a potholed court. Both sisters began competing before they were five.

Encourage your child to try out a variety of activities and clubs available at school. Being part of a school club or taking part in school-based activities not only fosters commitment on the part of both parent and child, it also cuts down on time parents spend traveling to take children to out-of-school clubs, and the child has more time to focus on school work when they return home.

Being a student council representative or a class captain can help your child develop leadership skills; being part of the school basketball or soccer team shows long-term commitment to a pursuit and can help your child learn social skills as they interact with others and develop positive relationships with them. Furthermore, team sports can help a child develop skills like following rules, respect for authority, and collaboration toward a common goal. Extracurricular activities can also instill in children qualities essential for lifelong success, such as a good work ethic, efficient time management, resilience, self-discipline, self-motivation, reliability, and willingness to take on responsibility.

Extracurricular activities can also raise a child's self-esteem and help them develop self-confidence. Children feel good about themselves when they excel at something. When children are unable to identify and celebrate their unique areas of strength, they see others as better than themselves, and this can bring about a sense of low self-worth. The fact is that not all children will pursue academics to the highest level; therefore, as parents it is important to get your child involved in other activities that will help them discover what they *are* good at. Excelling at a sport or playing a musical instrument has the potential to help your child believe that he can achieve in other areas. High self-esteem is one of the predictors of academic success.

Extracurricular activities keep children involved in doing something in their spare time that they actually enjoy. Furthermore, it helps to keep them from less productive activities, such as watching TV or playing video or computer games. Children easily get bored when they have nothing to do and will readily resort to spending an endless amount of time in front of the screen or hanging out with friends, sometimes even getting involved in dysfunctional activities. Extracurricular activities keep children busy and therefore out of trouble, especially during unsupervised periods like the gap between the end of school and the time when parents return from work.

Children who are involved in extracurricular activities are less likely to become addicted to bad habits like smoking and drinking and are deterred from anti-social behavior studies reveal. Anti-social and dysfunctional behaviors are linked to low self-esteem. A child who engages in an activity that they both enjoy and are good at will have higher self-esteem and self-respect, taking pride in their accomplishments, and most likely will not want to get involved in any activity that will tarnish their reputation.

Studies also show that children who are engaged in extracurricular activities have improved academic performance. The National Center for Education Statistics states: "Extracurricular activities provide a channel for reinforcing the lessons learned in the classroom, offering students the opportunity to apply academic skills in a real-world context, and are thus considered part of a well-rounded education."

Children who are engaged in extracurricular activities develop disciplines, routines, and positive attitudes that, when translated into their school work, can help them excel. Children who take part in sports are expected to live up to the high expectations of behavior, discipline, and respect for authority imposed by the coaches and the general rules of the game. Studies show a strong correlation between pupil behavior and academic performance. A well-behaved student is focused, assimilates more, and achieves better scores in assessments than a disruptive student.

Extracurricular activities add some zest to a student's college applications in many nations. Involvement in extracurricular activities is an important part of the university application process. It speaks loads about a student: it tells admissions officers and employers that the student is well-rounded and responsible. Top universities tend to favor well-rounded candidates who in their personal statements are able to demonstrate that they can commit to other activities that interest them.

In fact, students applying for places in top universities are in competition with countless other students who have top grades. Commitment and involvement in other areas can give one candidate the competitive edge over another, a bit like the icing on the cake. Studies in the UK show that the six extracurricular activities that add the most value to a personal statement are work experience, volunteering, Duke of Edinburgh, young enterprise, being in a sports team and fundraising.

Extracurricular activities also help prepare students to transition successfully into the workplace. Employers look for key qualities in employees, such as good communication skills, independent thinking, and responsibility. Children are able to acquire these skills by taking part in extracurricular activities.

BENEFITS OF PLAYING A MUSICAL INSTRUMENT

Have you considered encouraging your child to learn to play a musical instrument? The benefits include improving a child's overall ability to learn and achieve academically, but it can also position your child to take advantage of scholarship opportunities to independent schools and leading universities in many countries around the world. Moreover, with passion and practice, your child's talent can become an income-generating venture for them in the future. Research conducted by neuroscientists reveal that playing a musical instrument increases gray matter volume and makes neural connections between the two hemispheres of the brain, improving cognitive functions such as memory, problem-solving, sequential processing, and pattern-recognition.

Learning to play a musical instrument develops the part of the brain associated with sensory and motor skills. It equips children with the discipline and study habits that can help them do well in their studies and succeed in life. It can also improve the recall and retention of spoken words, because it develops the region of the brain responsible for verbal memory, the foundation for retaining information in all academic subjects. Moreover, it enhances working memory, the brain's ability to retain, control, and manipulate information, which is vital in performing higher order tasks like abstract reasoning and problem-solving.

Children who play a musical instrument perform better on math, reading, and writing assessments, because the parts of the brain used in processing these skills are strengthened through musical training. A 10-year study at University of California, Los Angeles involving 25,000 students show that music-making improves test scores in standardized tests, as well as in reading proficiency exams. Playing a musical instrument has also been shown to improve attention, perseverance, resilience, creativity, and self-esteem.

BENEFITS OF ARTS AND CRAFTS TO A CHILD'S DEVELOPMENT

Children derive immense benefit from engaging in arts and crafts, which provide opportunities to participate in both unstructured and structured activities that can improve imagination and creativity. Moreover, arts and crafts are low-cost and fun, activities that a child can do at home that will raise self-esteem and help them develop skills like problem-solving, critical thinking, and the ability to focus. They are also a good way of keeping children busy and away from addictive technology, especially younger children who usually do not have much homework.

Studies have indicated a very strong correlation between childhood engagement in the creative arts and measurable success in later life. Children who are exposed to a wide variety of arts and crafts are more likely to create unique inventions that are worthy of patents and to come up with innovative ideas robust enough to succeed in the marketplace.

Every non-academic activity that your child engages in can play a significant role in helping to build skills and abilities vital for their holistic development. These activities improve a child's overall sense of self-worth and develop disciplines that, when applied in their studies, will help them achieve academic excellence and success in their future lives. Invest your time in supporting your child's activities, while also ensuring that over-involvement doesn't hamper their academic performance.

ACTION POINTS

Write down four ways in which an involvement in extracurricular activities can benefit your child.

Describe steps you will take to ensure that extracurricular activities do not interfere with your child's schoolwork.

How can you find out which activities your child is passionate about?

Does your child have hobbies? If not, what are your plans for encouraging them to develop a new one?

What are the benefits to your child of playing a musical instrument?

____

____

____

What range of skills will your child develop while doing artwork?

____

____

____

GUIDE YOUR CHILD'S CHOICE OF CAREER

I have included this chapter in this book because I feel that after investing time and effort to follow the strategies outlined in this book to help your child excel in school, if you have my mindset, then you would want your high achiever to enjoy the rewards of your investment by finding themselves in an intellectually stimulating and financially rewarding career. Some high achievers have ended up pursuing careers with either low paying careers or careers with limited job prospects. Some have found themselves having to either work in fields unrelated to their qualifications or in unskilled jobs. A job simply involves working in the short term to earn money, but a *career* is the pursuit of a particular field of endeavor in a long-term progression toward a lifelong ambition. That's why making the right choice of career is crucial. Career choices can be a grey area, nevertheless, it remains an important aspect that can determine child's future outcomes. It is vital that you get involved in guiding them through the process of choosing a future career, one that will enable them to live a fulfilled life in the future. In this bonus chapter therefore, I discuss a range of considerations that might help you support your child to choose a career.

The Office for national statustics reveal that students in the UK graduate from university with debts averaging more than £44,000?

Nearly 40 percent of graduates are still looking for work six months after graduation, and a quarter are still unemployed after a year. Furthermore, 47 percent of graduates who find employment within six months are working in jobs that did not require a degree. Given that students graduate from university with huge debts, it is crucial to make informed choices, taking into consideration job prospects, financial reward and overall job satisfaction and fulfilment.

Globalization has altered the dynamics of the job market in certain fields, including relocation of many jobs to low-wage nations, causing a shortage of jobs in some sectors. As the world becomes a global village, competition for jobs has become fierce in certain sectors; job opportunities in certain sectors are open to applicants all over the world. A combination of qualifications and a broad range of other skills become important to position your child to compete successfully in the global market. Much more can be said about the topic of employability skills but to do that would mean going beyond the scope of this book.

A financially rewarding career can help your child to accumulate savings that can be used to start a business or pursue their dreams. Money is not everything, but a financially rewarding job will provide your child a comfortable lifestyle, enable them to enjoy the good things that life affords, help them send their children to the best schools, enable them to support charitable causes of their choice, and can allow them to support the furtherance of the gospel, just to name a few of the benefits.

The importance of financial stability in your children cannot be overemphasized. While it's true that people perform best and are more likely to excel in areas they are passionate about, parents might need to err on the side of caution in allowing their children to simply go with whatever they are passionate about. It's not rare for a child to become disinterested in something in which they previously had a strong interest. Sometimes, because of the challenges of turning passion into a successful business venture, a child's area of passion might not be financially rewarding enough to offer them the lifestyle they might desire.

SOME FACTORS THAT CAN INFLUENCE A CHILD'S PASSION

The media

On television we see musicians, actors, and all kinds of sports stars who may not have gone to college, but who are making millions of dollars a year. Television also portrays people who have gone from nothing to celebrity status just by appearing on reality TV shows or by getting married to a rich partner. The media can influence children to believe that they can be successful by pursuing one of these paths to success.

The media also shows very successful people who have followed their passions and achieved great success. Children can easily be influenced by the successful people they see on TV, take them as their role models, and seek to become like them. It's human nature to seek to pursue the path of least resistance. It's important for parents to teach their children that achieving success in some of these ways is the exception rather than the rule, and that the majority of people who set off to pursue their dreams in the sports or entertainment industry never achieve fame and fortune.

Teachers

Teachers can pick up on skills and abilities that their students have, since they spend so much time with them. Sometimes teachers can point out skills in their students and encourage them to develop them. Because a lot of children believe in what their teachers say about them, many actually consider their teachers' suggestions.

Parents

Parents are able to influence their children's passions and career choices either intentionally or inadvertently. Parents who have successful careers that have enabled them to afford a comfortable lifestyle are more likely to influence their children to pursue financially rewarding careers, while parents who own successful businesses are likely to encourage their children to pursue entrepreneurship in the future. Moreover, children sometimes grow up idealizing their parent's professions.

Peers

Humans in a lot of cases are a product of their environment. The environment in which a person grows can influence their mindset, behaviour, habits, attitudes, and even their understanding of different aspects of life. Children spend about 6-7 hours daily in school, during term time. They interact and form close friendships with other children and in the process, can influence each other in different ways, even in terms of aspiration and career choices.

It's important for parents to guide and support their children's career choices. Start to discuss their future with your child early and often. As much as you want to get involved in your child's career choice, it is important to avoid forcing a child to pursue a career they have no interest in. I strongly believe that any child can be successful in any career they pursue, provided they have a good understanding of principles of success like excellence, hard work, persistence, resilience, an ability to learn from mistakes, and a thirst for ongoing self-learning to improve areas in which they're deficient. These principles, not in the curriculum and not taught in school, are the responsibility of parents to instill.

SOME CONSIDERATIONS WHEN SUPPORTING AND GUIDING YOUR CHILD'S CAREER CHOICE

Your child's natural abilities

Parents are the best judges of their children's unique skills, talents, and abilities. (I won't focus on sporting talents in this chapter, since I have dealt with it in the previous one.) Parents should do all they can to support their children in developing these skills. If your child shows an interest in a specific area of science, for example, you can help him explore and strengthen it by encouraging him to read books and watch TV documentaries in that area, and visit science museums and activity centers that are relevant to that interest. You can also encourage them to carry out independent research on Google and YouTube, rewarding their efforts in gaining knowledge of the topic. The same applies to practical skills like baking, hairdressing, plumbing, etc., since practice makes perfect in any pursuit, and the better a child becomes at a skill, the greater the likelihood of their interest continuing to grow.

Research your child's careers of interest

Children tend to have a number of careers they may be interested in pursuing. Therefore, it's necessary to guide them in making informed choices by researching each career. As you do so, pay attention to skills needed, entry requirements into the best colleges for each specific career, and how work patterns might affect lifestyle. Avoid hindering your child from pursuing a career because they apparently do not have the full set of skills required for it. Skills like many other attributes in life can be learnt and developed given the right mindset and motivation. For example, a career as a pilot entails traveling and being away from family for a few days at a time, depending on the destination. It is important for your child to consider whether they would be happy being away from family on a regular basis. Look into job prospects and career progression within the specific industry as well as salaries. Some professions have greater prospects than others. For example, a student in the medical or teaching profession is likely to get a job before the end of his final year of studies, unlike many professions.

Speak to someone in your child's field of interest

Find someone who is working in your child's chosen profession who can chat with them and give them a realistic view of the intricacies of the job. This will help the child to identify skills they might need to develop or experiences they might need to acquire prior to applying at a suitable college, as well as helping them to determine whether they would be happy in that job.

Financial reward

I've heard a lot of people say, "Money isn't everything." I consider a financially rewarding career as a reward for the parents' investment in their children's life in terms of time and resources. Discuss the need for financial rewards when choosing a career. You can carry out a Google search of rankings for careers and corresponding wages. I find it rather unfortunate and consider it a waste of potential when children who have consistently been high achievers have ended up in low-paying jobs through poor career decisions.

Many children have a shallow perception of real-life financial commitments and, as a result, they make career decisions that will leave them perpetually in a tight financial situation. Help your child to gain a realistic view of how far typical earnings can go toward meeting a person's basic needs. Discuss with them such things as typical weekly expenditures on housing expenses, taxes, utility bills, tithes, transportation costs, food, savings, and leisure. Although there are many jobs that provide personal satisfaction and financial reward, some professions are much more financially rewarding than others. According to the UK Office of National Statistics, among the top 20 highest paid jobs are the chief executives, senior officials and managers of various institutions, brokers, pilots, medical practitioners, legal professionals, and workers in the financial sector.

The ideal for any child is to study at one of the leading prestigious colleges or universities. Alternatively, parents should support their children in researching the universities that are renowned for providing the highest standard of training their child's chosen course of study. Attending such an institution increases your child's prospects of getting a job in that field, since employers in various industries are aware of which colleges offer the best training in their fields.

In the grand scheme of things, a parent's role is to lovingly guide their child's choice of career, helping them make well-informed decisions that will provide lifelong rewards. People generally excel, experience a greater sense of fulfilment and satisfaction and express themselves optimally in areas of their passion. Encourage your child to aim for financially rewarding sectors within the fields they are passionate about. Where the prospects are limited within your child's area of passion, you could encourage them to pursue another financially rewarding career they might be interested in while developing their passion alongside. In future the high earning job might provide the financial leverage to help them develop their passion into a money generating venture. In whatever way you get involved in laying the right foundation for your child's future, pray and carry your child with love all along the way.

ACTION POINTS

When is it best to start talking to your child about career choices?

____

____

____

What are some of the challenges of the job market that you would consider when guiding your child's choice of career?

Write down three things that can influence your child's choice of career.

What is your child's passion?

Are they considering a career in their area of passion?

What are the key factors you would consider in guiding your child's choice of career?

____

____

____

Pauline Limen is the founder and CEO of *Star Reachers*, an organisation that actively seeks to equip parents with effective tools to help children aspire to academic excellence and success. Pauline Limen is an educator, an academic achievement strategist, a parent mentor and a Certified Life Coach for children and teenagers. With a wealth of experience working with young people and parents, she is passionate about teaching and has twelve successful years in secondary education in the UK.

An inspiring motivational speaker on a mission to combat prevailing underachievement, Pauline shows parents easy strategies they can implement at home to support academic excellence and success in life for their children. Pauline believes that a good education and career can change the trajectory of a person's life, open up doors of opportunity for them and guarantee upward social mobility.

Pauline believes strongly that each child has unique skills, talents and abilities and that through strategic parental involvement, children could achieve their full potential. She has delivered a range of high-impact practical parent and youth empowerment seminars and workshops at conferences, churches, community groups and schools. She has also delivered several inspirational keynote speeches and has been a guest on several radio shows.

PAULINE PANI LIMEN

HELPING PARENTS RAISE HIGH ACHIEVERS

SEMINARS AND WORKSHOPS ARE AVAILABLE FOR PARENTS AND CARERS

WORKSHOPS ARE AVAILABLE FOR TEENAGERS

MENTORING IS AVAILABLE FOR PARENTS AND TEENAGERS

LIFE COACHING IS AVAILABLE FOR CHILDREN AND TEENAGERS IN SCHOOLS

KEYNOTE TALKS AND PRESENTATIONS AVAILABLE FOR EVENTS

CONSULTANCY SERVICES AVAILABLE FOR PUBLIC AND PRIVATE SECTOR ORGANISATIONS

FOR MORE INFORMATION ABOUT PAULINE LIMEN, STAR REACHERS AND OUR SERVICES PLEASE VISIT THE WEBSITE AT WWW.STARREACHERS.CO.UK OR CONTACT US AT info@starreachers.co.uk

FOLLOW US ON:

FACEBOOK : https://www.facebook.com/
Star-Reachers-509815579122730/
TWITTER : HTTPS://TWITTER.COM/PAULINELIMEN
LINKEDIN : PAULINE LIMEN

Note from the Publisher

Are you a first time author?

Not sure how to proceed to get your book published?
Want to keep all your rights and all your royalties?
Want it to look as good as a Top 10 publisher?
Need help with editing, layout, cover design?
Want it out there selling in 90 days or less?

Visit our website for some exciting new options!

Printed in Great Britain
by Amazon.co.uk, Ltd.,
Marston Gate.